BETTER HOMES AND GARDENS®

New
Cottage Style

A **Better Homes and Gardens** Book
An Imprint of

NOTE TO THE READERS: Due to differing conditions, tools, and individual skills, John Wiley & Sons, Inc., assumes no responsibility for any damages, injuries suffered, or losses incurred as a result of following the information published in this book. Before beginning any project, review the instructions carefully, and if any doubts or questions remain, consult local experts or authorities. Because codes and regulations vary greatly, you always should check with authorities to ensure that your project complies with all applicable local codes and regulations. Always read and observe all of the safety precautions provided by manufacturers of any tools, equipment, or supplies, and follow all accepted safety procedures.

BETTER HOMES AND GARDENS® MAGAZINE
Gayle Goodson Butler
Executive Vice President and Editor in Chief
Oma Blaise Ford
Executive Editor
Michael D. Belknap
Creative Director

BETTER HOMES AND GARDENS® NEW COTTAGE STYLE
Editor: Paula Marshall
Contributing Editor: Jody Garlock
Contributing Designer: Gayle Schadendorf
Contributing Copy Editor: Nancy McClimen
Cover Photographer: Kim Cornelison
Contributing Photo Researcher: Cathy Long

SPECIAL INTEREST MEDIA
Editorial Director: Gregory H. Kayko
Content Core Director, Home: Jill Waage
Deputy Content Core Director, Home: Karman Hotchkiss
Managing Editor: Doug Kouma
Art Director: Gene Rauch
Group Editor: Lacey Howard
Copy Chief: Jennifer Speer Ramundt
Business Director: Janice Croat

MEREDITH NATIONAL MEDIA GROUP
President: Tom Harty
Executive Vice President: Doug Olson

MEREDITH CORPORATION
Chairman and Chief Executive Officer: Stephen M. Lacy

JOHN WILEY AND SONS, INC.
Vice President and Publisher: Cindy Kitchel
Acquisitions Editor: Pam Mourouzis
Production Director: Diana Cisek
Manufacturing Coordinator: Kimberly Kiefer

Welcome

Comfortable. Relaxed. Inviting. Is it any wonder cottage style remains a favorite? But today's looks move beyond these timeless traits. Colors are fresher, collections are sparer, and rooms are more personal than ever. We're so enamored with the smart new looks that we want to share them with you. In our House Tours and Room Views, you'll gain a bounty of ideas to refresh your home. Feeling DIYish? Try your hand at the simple projects in our Notebook. Every house—regardless of architectural style—holds the promise of becoming the cottage you love. So come on in...let's decorate!

contents

everyday living

Cottage style has never been easier to live with. Streamlined and welcoming modern elements, this hybrid look is at home virtually anywhere.

SPRINKLED IN
Color has the power to transform anything it touches. On the banquette, four solid-color pillows update the look of cushions and pillows sewn from recycled coffee bags.

color it happy

Juicy pops of attention-getting hues work their magic on this home, infusing it with a playful spirit that has a fresh-and easy feel.

Color speaks volumes about a home. It instantly conveys a message and evokes a feeling. With citrus hues—oranges, limes, and yellows—and tropical blues, this home is as energetic and confident as it is warm and welcoming.

The color punch delivers the moment visitors knock on the tangerine front door. Inside, an abstract painting that inspired the uplifting palette draws the eyes down the entry hall into the living room. The juicy hues turn up throughout the home—on a vintage coffee table, glass bottles, even a bedroom ceiling. Slightly varying the shades gives each room its own personality. Tangerine, for example, turns rusty orange on the back porch.

For all its happy color, though, the home still plays it smart. Foundation pieces are neutral—a perfect choice for anyone who craves color but also wants the flexibility to change the mood.

KICK-BACK CASUAL
Washable slipcovers and seagrass carpet relax the living room. The vintage coffee table, with wood showing beneath worn turquoise paint, bridges the room's neutral pieces and the bright colors inspired by the painting above the mantel.

CURTAIN CALL

top left **Stationary curtain panels sewn from wide horizontal bands of coral and white linen bring playful style to the traditional dining room.**

EASY VIGNETTE

top right **Glass bottles are a natural accessory in cottage decorating. Here, decanters and a pitcher used as a vase form a striking display on an accent table.**

VISUAL VARIETY

middle left **A mix of textures in fabrics, accent tables, and accessories enlivens the living room's neutral pieces. Patterned pillows add life and tie into the home's color scheme.**

KEEPING IT CLASSIC

middle right **With an apron-front sink, a tongue-and-groove backsplash and ceiling, and wavy glass on cabinet doors, the kitchen appears reminiscent of an earlier era. Countertops made from crushed oyster shells add beach-inspired texture.**

FIRST IMPRESSION

bottom **For an in-a-day exterior spruce-up, paint the front door. Here, the tangerine door injects tropical flair into the traditional home. Blue-gray shutters and a wraparound porch give the new home a vintage beach-cottage look.**

ENTRY INTRIGUE
above left **In the wide center hallway, floor-to-ceiling bookcases tucked under the staircase follow the lead of vintage homes, where built-ins and niches fill nooks and crannies. Picture lights add more character and illuminate photographs and collections displayed on the shelves.**

ENERGY BOOST
above right **To keep a bedroom restful, shift bold color from walls to the ceiling. In the master bedroom, walls with just a hint of color temper the boldness of the teal-painted ceiling. Teal stripes on the table skirt and draperies are trimmed with frayed burlap—a small detail that brings unassuming cottage style into the more traditional room.**

Color is a simple way to bring something personal to your home. Even if you're drawn to neutrals, a few hits of a favorite hue will add warmth and make your home seem more like you.

PORCH PIZZAZZ
Graphic pillows jazz up
the screen porch, while a
floor lamp with a clear
base fades away. The
vintage table and benches
wear their original paint.

COLLECTED APPEAL
In the living room, an antique post becomes a plant stand and an old drawer is repurposed as a magazine holder. A charcoal-gray slipcover on the sofa helps the room strike a balance between masculine and feminine.

savoring small

It doesn't take big rooms to deliver big personality. This home shows ideas for living large and using vintage treasures to uplift snug spaces.

In room after room, this character-rich home makes the point that it's not the size of a house that matters, but what you do with it. At about 1,200 square feet, the home isn't large—rooms tend to be basic 11-foot squares. But you barely notice that, thanks to surprises that engage the eye. In the living room, a pitcher holds an unexpected bouquet: artist's paintbrushes instead of flowers. In the dining room, a closet door swings open to reveal a bar, cleverly created from stacked vintage suitcases.

The makeshift bar is among the space-stretching tricks that ultimately make the home more livable. Another nod to livability: grain sacks draped over upholstered chairs to add depth and make them more pet-friendly. Subdued colors contribute a sense of ease. Grays, creams, and taupes show the less-feminine side of cottage style. In fact, this home seems to strike a perfect balance— gender-neutral, cozy, and full of intrigue.

METAL MIX
Burnished metals give the home a sense of age. In the snug dining room, tarnished trophy-shape vases, a zinc tabletop, and a bronze-finish chandelier complement the bronze knobs and hardware used throughout the house.

DOUBLED-UP CLOSET

left When space is at a premium, get creative. In the dining room, a coat closet shifts into a bar for entertaining guests. The suitcases provide storage space, while a serving tray creates a level surface atop the stool-and-suitcase setup. Vintage wallpaper inspired the equestrian accents; the iron horseshoe visually ties in with a hanging rod (not shown), left in place so coats can easily go back.

ON DISPLAY

above left Dark taupe paint sets off collections and accentuates the beaded-board backs on the dining room built-ins. Ironstone gravy boats used as accessories mix with an antique propeller and other treasures. Wood and metal boxes are decorative and functional, storing paper and office supplies.

CUSHY COMFORT

above The window seat's sink-into-it allure comes from two lumbar pillows tucked into vintage German laundry bags. This no-sew version looks more casual than one boxy custom-fit cushion. Paint colors on the built-ins reverse the scheme of the upholstered chairs, which are covered in off-white linen and trimmed in brown leather.

Try this!
Age furniture by sanding paint off corners, drawers, and areas that get the most wear.

SVELTE STORAGE

Bring a slim console or sofa table into a small kitchen to gain extra function. Here, an antique console with heavily worn paint provides storage and can also be set up as a buffet. The table is an easy-access station for everyday linens and kitchen twine. Double the storage with a table that has a bottom shelf. Cookbooks fill this console's shelf; Roseville pottery bowls serve as bookends.

TICKTOCK
above **Vintage clocks, including one shaped like a teapot, mingle with dishes on the kitchen's open shelving, adding charming personality.**

SQUEEZE PLAY
right **An old slate-top lab table used as a breakfast bar and prep space is just the right fit in the tiny kitchen. Stock cabinets from a home center—painted and topped with butcher block—greatly improve the room's function; before, there were no cabinets. Open shelves provide storage and display space. A vintage metal clipboard becomes an eye-level recipe holder.**

Cook up personality in the kitchen. Display a collection—such as cookbooks or clocks. Potted plants or herbs you can snip off to flavor dishes are refreshing touches.

GENTLE TOUCH

opposite **Gray damask wallpaper in the master bedroom creates an elegant backdrop for rustic pieces, including the farm sign above the bed. A random pattern gives the antique quilt a more modern look.**

ARTFUL CORNER

above left **An awkward stair-landing space becomes a cozy sitting area with bonus storage. The old Mexican cabinet—perhaps once a washstand—adds fun color. The antique art piece above it was likely used in a church or other building to represent the Trinity; here, it adds graphic flair.**

URBAN RENEWAL

above right **Restoring the porch and uncovering the front door's sidelights brought the 1842 Greek Revival home closer to its original state. Cedar siding painted warm gray hints at the interior color.**

TWO-TONE TUB

right **Taupe paint updates the outside of the old claw-foot tub, formerly painted pink. For a quick makeover, primer and latex paint were used. For a longer-lasting option, have a cast-iron tub professionally refinished; it might require sandblasting to remove excess layers of paint. On upper walls, gray-and-white-striped wallpaper adds subtle pattern.**

MAKE AN ENTRANCE
Painted black, the front
door and trim—along
with a black lantern and
mailbox—give the facade
of the 1800s farmhouse a
little punch.

country soul

This home's doors open to the landscape that inspired its reinvention.
Despite its updated interior, the home is still an old farmhouse at heart.

A mix of old charm and new shine is the driving force of cottage style today. It's also what drove the reinvention of this 1800s farmhouse to bring it into modern times suited for an active family.

Wooden windows, period hardware and light fixtures, and reclaimed Douglas fir floors retain the home's charm. Salvaged timber and stone play up the country setting, giving a sense that items have been brought in from outdoors.

The shine comes from larger windows, French doors, and an updated white kitchen that opens to the dining room and patio— all giving the home breathing room conducive to modern living. Fabrics and furniture simultaneously reflect sophistication and ease, as does the color scheme. Soothing whites and soft neutrals provide the calm that's perfect for countering busy lifestyles.

WARM AND COZY

opposite **A stone fireplace and aged-timber mantel give the living room a down-to-earth look. The rustic coffee table is an antique desk with legs cut to the appropriate height. A cozy mix of plaid, leather, and linen fabrics gives the room put-your-feet-up style.**

COUNTRY CHARM

top **A lush garden encircles the home for a welcoming first impression. Dormers detail the exterior and provide a bit more elbowroom inside.**

PHOTO EFFECTS

middle right **Black-and-white photographs are a striking and affordable way to fill wall space above a sofa. Use software to convert color images to black and white, and place in black frames with wide white mats for a graphic look. Grouped, the photos read as one large art piece.**

BRANCH OUT

bottom right **A tree-limb coatrack that reflects the home's nature-inspired theme is functional and sculptural—and slim enough to fit into a corner near the front door.**

STAYING IN TOUCH

far right **Wide doorways make an easy connection among the dining room, entry, and living room. A fully open layout would have been too modern for the old home.**

WELCOME CONTRAST
left Sculptural chairs dress up the casual dining table. Built-ins with glass-panel doors resemble a hutch. A black granite serving ledge between the cabinets echoes the kitchen countertops.

HIDDEN POTENTIAL
above left Extra storage space can come from unexpected places. In the kitchen, shelves built beneath the stairway provide tucked-away storage that keeps the walkway clear. French baskets in the same color but different sizes ensure the shelves look tidy.

FRESH UPDATE
above Sliding pocket doors open the renovated kitchen to a secondary dining area on a side patio. Honed granite, a subway tile backsplash, and glass-front cabinets add a classic look.

EASY INTERACTION
With a wall removed, the kitchen and dining room become one large space that fits today's casual lifestyles. A chalkboard front turns the refrigerator into a message board. The island is an antique marble-top cupboard.

updating a farmhouse
Consider these tips for modernizing an old house.

Assess the layout. In the past, boxy rooms with little detail dominated farmhouses. To make a home seem less confined, widen doorways or open closed-in rooms by removing a wall. A completely open plan, though, will likely seem out of place.

Soften the palette. Scrubbable painted walls, all in the same off-white, made farmhouses easy to maintain. Today, the palette is softer and varied. Try new neutrals, such as pale gray or khaki.

Mix furniture. Farmhouses were built to be hardworking, and furniture followed suit. Function is still important, but so is variety. Avoid too many antiques, which can make a house feel like a museum. An eclectic collection works well.

BUNKING IN

opposite **Take advantage of the nooks and crannies old houses offer. Here, bunk beds tuck into an alcove. Painted white to match the background, they almost look like they're built in.**

GROOMING STATION

above left **In the master bath, a dormer creates space to tuck in a vanity. Open shelves with rattan baskets offer easy access and keep the look casual.**

LAYERED INTEREST

above right **A pedestal sink keeps the bathroom on the classic side. Backed by a built-in cabinet, it has the functionality of a traditional sink vanity. Sconces, rather than a bar-style light, add elegance. A tufted chair and ceramic stool create a little living area in the bath, which is large for its era.**

COLLECTED LOOK

right **The master bedroom is pulled together but not matchy. Shades of red unify fabrics on the bed and chair. Mismatched furniture has gathered-over-time appeal.**

CLEAR CONNECTION
Ultramodern chairs
scoot up to a rustic table
in the dining area of this
renovated cottage. Small
pots of succulents on the
table bring the outside in.
With the glass doors
open, the room offers
fresh-air dining.

modern comfort

White walls, sleek furniture, and walls of glass might sound like the makings of a contemporary home. But look closely, and you'll discover the cottage within.

Cottage and modern hardly seem like words that go together. But they're the perfect pairing to describe what's happening with cottage style today. This renovated home, having evolved from a no-frills and closed-in 1940s beach cottage to an airy and comfy home that can handle a bevy of activity, inside and out, reflects the trend.

Sleek furnishings, such as molded melamine dining chairs, give the decor its modern attitude. White walls can read either coastal cottage or cool contemporary. A spacious patio is set up with a dining area, sitting area, and relaxing spa tub, taking full advantage of square footage outdoors.

Even when the home's cottage style takes a modern turn, it doesn't stray from its classic roots—built-ins and dormers for character, windows that catch outdoor views, and rooms truly meant for living.

IN THE DETAILS
Subway tile, glass-front cabinets, and a paneled island and ceiling bring vintage flavor to the kitchen and dining area. The zinc counter topping the island will develop a patina over time (unlike more common stainless steel). Upholstery tacks detail the counter; the points were cut off, then the heads were glued to the edge of the countertop. Glass doors that open the dining area to the patio and a wide window in the kitchen's desk area heighten the indoor-outdoor connection.

modern comfort

STARTING OVER

left Ceiling beams hint at the home's origin as a 1940s beach cottage. Painted white to blend with the ceiling, they have a modern look. Formerly the living room, this space is set up as a game room and art gallery. Framed art casually leaning on the long mantel creates a change-at-will display.

CONTRAST COUNTS

opposite In the living room, woven baskets play against the smooth wood of the built-in, visually warming the modern scheme with texture. A Roman shade looks fresh and modern in plain white fabric and hung on a rod from curtain rings.

LESS IS MORE
above left **A limited palette of tone-on-tone neutrals and pattern-free fabrics contributes to the master bedroom's tranquil look.**

PATIO LIFE
left **Modern touches carry onto the patio with clean-lined white furniture and a spa tub. Silvery accent tables add a bit of glamour. The stone fireplace and bluestone pavers ensure a warm and welcoming ambience.**

STANDING OUT
above right **Use furniture and accessories to accentuate a room's architectural assets. Here, a pair of bright-color chairs and bouquet of flowers draw attention to the dormer and its interesting angles.**

BATH SPLASH
A garden stool placed by the tub becomes a handy and space-saving table to hold bath-time essentials. Sheer white curtains add a layer of softness and blend into the background for a clean, spa-like look.

PRESENT TENSE
A reclaimed barn beam for the mantel and penny tile on the fireplace surround give the renovated family room old-fashioned appeal. The dogwood print hides the flat-panel TV, recessed into the wall.

house blend

As this family-friendly bungalow shows, it's possible to have the charm of an old home and still keep up with the demands of modern living.

Fitting a modern lifestyle into an old home can seem like a case of square peg in round hole. This renovated 1923 Craftsman bungalow manages to work it all in— easy flow, space for computers, storage—without sacrificing charm.

Removing a few interior walls allowed better connections among the family room, kitchen, and dining room. The kitchen fits the same footprint as the original space but works better now with a two-tier island—one level for prepping, the other for doing homework, working on a laptop, or just chatting.

The secret to success when modernizing an old home? Keep the past in mind. Knee walls with pillars ensure the open plan isn't too open. Window seats are an old-house feature, but outfitted with drawers they offer a place to hide away today's gadgetry. Such respect for the past makes for a win for the present.

SHARED STRATEGY
An oversize drum lampshade and sleek chairs with mismatched slipcovers add a modern hint to the home's classic architecture. The lesson: Clean lines always mix.

STYLISHLY SHIELDED
above left In an open plan, a tiered island helps solve the **problem** of dirty dishes and cooking messes being on display. Here, subway tile covers the front, giving the modern island old style.

DOUBLE-DUTY SPACE
above middle Tucked next to the family room, the office and playroom get daily use—enough to justify converting a seldom-used bedroom.

STOCK UP
above right A hutch loaded with storage options is the kitchen's focal point. Although it looks like an expensive custom piece, it's actually stock cabinetry creatively configured.

PET PROJECT
right A custom doghouse abuts the soft window seating in the breakfast room—a pretty and practical alternative to a freestanding kennel. Drawers in the window seat store pet supplies.

Try this!
Outfit an interior window or transom with leaded glass for an artful look with old-house style.

SIZED RIGHT

right **A barn beam table and a stool with a hand-hewn look take the place of a traditional nightstand and suit the low height of the bed. The interior window above channels natural light into a walk-in closet.**

TILE STYLE

opposite **Even when they're all white, a mix of tiles adds interest. In the master bathroom, basket-weave floor tile and penny tile on the tub surround lend luxurious period style. Subway tile—another old-time favorite—details the shower walls.**

update for the times

This old home's shift to modern living is filled with ideas you can apply to yours.

Lift the mood. Mixing in white with stained wood instantly updates and brightens a home. This house introduced white by way of painted pillars, a hutch and subway tile in the kitchen, and cabinets in the family room. The white keeps the oak and cherry details from becoming heavy-handed.

Waste no space. It's better to give rooms a new use than to let them sit idle. A formal dining room could become a second TV-watching space, or, as in this home, a spare bedroom could be an office and playroom. Think of it this way: Do what works 90 percent of the time, and improvise the other 10 percent.

Update colors. Dated colors drag a house down. Establish a fresh palette and use variations of it throughout the home to tie everything together. A soothing wash of pale greens and blues keeps this home fresh.

A barn becomes a character-rich backdrop for the patio near this 1900 farmhouse. Stainless-steel folding chairs that are a take on antique bistro chairs modernize the space.

a fresh start

Early-20th-century farmhouses have always offered opportunities for creating a cottage look. The changeup? Fun, modern touches are welcome, too.

Old farmhouses are known for their no-nonsense attitudes. They get right to the point, with straightforward exteriors and no-frills interiors. Even in renovated farmhouses, the decor often harkens to the past, with primitive pieces and a somewhat sparse appearance that respects the hardworking lifestyle that produced the architectural style.

With this 1900 farmhouse, though, what you might expect isn't necessarily what you get. Hints of modern—a graphic rug here, a contemporary chair there—inject a playful attitude. Bright color freshens up familiar farmhouse pieces, such as cane chairs and a rag rug. The traditional layout—rooms are rooms, not one big open space—ensures there's an old-fashioned sense of home, albeit with a slightly modern point of view.

a fresh start

making it modern

Give any room a style lift by bringing in a few fresh touches.

Don't go overboard. Layer in modern elements after you've established the room's foundation. Pillows and rugs are good places to start, because they're easy to change if you want to revert back. Use super-edgy contemporary forms sparingly; they make a big statement.

Have fun with color. Breathe life into a room with colorful accents. Citrus hues, such as yellow, orange, and lime, are hip yet full of cottage cheerfulness.

Balance it out. A rule of thumb: When you use something old, put something modern with it. An antique dresser, for example, looks instantly fresher with a chrome lamp on it rather than a lantern. The same rule applies to shapes: Pair sleek with curvy.

WORKED IN

opposite To accommodate a range of activities, look for ways for a room to multitask. In the living room, a side table becomes a space-saving computer desk. A contemporary chair ensures the space doesn't look "officey."

FORMAL ABANDON

above left A mismatched table and chairs and a graphic rug put a friendly face on the dining room.

LOUNGE AROUND

above right An out-of-the-way corner of the living room becomes a tranquil reading and relaxation nook, with just a chaise longue, floor lamp, and small table.

ON TREND

right Small accessories allow guilt-free playing around with trendy colors and patterns. Touches of gray—on pillows, the rug, throw, and reflective tables—tone down the living room's vivid hues.

a fresh start

TRIED AND TRUE
The renovated home bucks the trend toward open spaces with a kitchen that's separate from other rooms—and retains a classic look. Beams and open shelves have paint rubbed off for a rustic whitewashed look. Open shelves keep dishes in easy reach.

GATHERING PLACE

above left **With a sofa, the breakfast room (formerly a porch) becomes a gathering spot for more than just meals. Leaving windows undressed simplifies the space. Bright colors modernize the look of the dining chairs and rag rug.**

IN HARMONY

above right **A graphic duvet and pillows take the serene toile bed from traditional to modern. The style mix works because the duvet is bold enough to dominate; the toile fades away so the two patterns don't compete. At the end of the bed, an antique table becomes a drop zone and display space, taking the place of the usual bench.**

EYE CATCHER

right **A room doesn't have to have a riot of color to be colorful. In the mostly neutral guest bedroom, a turquoise lamp adds a single spark of bright color. Bringing in other bold hues would only diminish its impact.**

classic looks

Slipcovers, painted furniture, and timeworn treasures speak the language. These homes present cottage icons in new ways—and prove you can't go wrong with tradition.

OCEANS AWAY
White walls welcome any accent colors. Old ceiling tiles painted ocean blue and sea green and hung as art launch this home's beachy scheme. A mirror rimmed with salvaged wood pieces adds more cottage character.

seeing the white

Stripped-down color—white, white, and more white—and streamlined furnishings
prove that a blend of cottage and modern can be forward yet still timeless.

Light, airy, and pristine, white-on-white schemes
have long been a favorite in cottage-style decorating. But there's
nothing old-school about the look. In this sun-bleached 1960s
saltbox, clean-lined furniture and lacquered pieces mix with
cottage icons such as slipcovered sofas and whitewashed antiques
to give rooms a crisp and modern edge. Well-edited accessories—
some of them salvaged gems—contribute to the fresh look, too.

The real beauty of splashing on white is simplicity. It instantly
brightens, makes rooms look bigger, and goes with everything.

To keep a white scheme from looking like a blank canvas or
veering toward ultramodern starkness, introduce hits of color. In
this home, a range of blues and sea greens evokes a by-the-beach
feeling. Texture—whether in a seagrass rug or a furry pillow—is
another key to warming up white.

seeing the white

RELAXED FIT
above A lacquered coffee table—topped with an ice bucket used as a vase—streamlines the eclectic furniture mix in the living room. French accent chairs are relaxed, with new white canvas upholstery and white paint rubbed onto their legs and frames. In the corner, a pine armoire received a similar whitewashing, with wet paint rubbed off to allow some of the original finish to show.

ART SMARTS
right For interesting and affordable art, get creative. Vintage algae sun prints downloaded from a library's collection (*digitalgallery.nypl.org*) double as freebie art that, framed in white, fits the airy scheme. A rusty seahorse weather vane becomes cottage-worthy sculpture when displayed on a wood block.

SHIFT CHANGE
opposite A seldom-used dining room becomes a TV room—proving that a space doesn't have to be used for its original purpose. The mirrored art piece is a do-it-yourself take on a trumeau mirror. For a similar look, scratch the back of a mirror to age it. Adhere the mirror, decorative medallions, and trim to plywood. Paint the piece white, rubbing off some of the wet paint.

living with white

Keep a white room livable and looking fresh with these tips.

Temper it. Light-reflecting white can be hard on the eyes, so vary the shades used and add texture. Remember that the more windows in a room, the brighter the white will look.

Pick the right paint. Give furniture—and even accessories such as trays—a modern lacquered look with glossy-sheen paint. For a less showy look, use flat paint. To age a piece, rub off wet paint so part of the layer beneath shows; focus on areas that would naturally show wear, such as those around dresser knobs.

Be realistic. White looks clean, but it won't stay clean. So choose slipcovers that can be washed and bleached. For floors and cabinetry, use oil-base paint; it's durable and can be washed—and a good choice for things that get heavy use.

seeing the white

NATURAL SELECTION
Texture brings visual
relief to a white scheme.
A woven rug and raw-
wood table—the top
is a door—are light
enough to keep the
breakfast room bright.

Try this!

A sleek worktable from a restaurant supply store is an airy alternative to an island.

GLASS ACT

above right Upper cabinet doors outfitted with glass visually open the small kitchen. If clear glass makes dishes too front and center, choose frosted glass or line the insides of the doors with curtains, using a sheer fabric for translucency.

CURB APPEAL

middle right Cedar shingles and starfish visible through the front door's transom give the renovated home cottage flourish.

FRAME THE VIEW

below right Pieces of driftwood nailed to the frame and painted white create a beachy take on a starburst mirror.

MINI MUDROOM

far right Function trumps authenticity in the mudroom-inspired area, formerly a windowless closet. Easy-to-install panels that resemble beaded board cover lower walls; the prepainted panels wipe clean. Closet shelves were repurposed into a bench and a platform that organizes shoes and helps keep the floor clean.

seeing the white

CLEAN SWEEP
Blue accents mellow to gray in the bedroom. A clean-lined end table stands in for a heavy-looking nightstand. (Place a basket or bin between table legs to store books and magazines.) Canvas curtains add breezy cottage style, and grommeted tops give them modern flair. Hanging the rods close to the ceiling visually lengthens the windows.

LAYERED LOOK

below **Layers** give a room depth. The dresser, with white paint showing from under the gray top coat, displays the timeworn quality cottage style embraces. A mirror and painting propped rather than hung offer casual ease. A stack of books and a decorative box topped with a shell heighten interest.

VINTAGE INFLUENCE

right There's no rule that says a cabinet-style vanity has to fill a long wall in a bathroom. With two pedestal sinks and a sleek chrome étagère that uses vertical space, the bathroom melds cottage charm with modern function. Instead of a light bar hung above the mirrors, ceiling-mounted schoolhouse lights illuminate the space.

TUCKED IN
An awkward under-eaves space becomes an inviting focal point with a bed dressed in pinks and greens. A simple canopy softens the setting. Create a similar look with sheer fabric and towel rings or hooks.

sweet dreams

With pretty pastels and flirty ruffles, this home exudes quintessential cottage style. It's soft, romantic, and inviting—yet updated so it's not frozen in time.

Today's streamlined cottage style doesn't mean giving up soft pastels and feminine flourishes. It simply means knowing when to say when. Pink? Sure; just add splashes of vibrant color such as apple green so it's not so saccharine. Ruffles? Let them flow, then offset the frills with clean-lined touches.

Sweet but simple is the mantra in this renovated 1920s cottage. A palette that includes soft pink and green supplies the sweet, while white-painted walls and floors keep backdrops simple. Accessories are a mix of both characteristics. Shells picked up on beaches and family china create personal displays that didn't cost money but are filled with meaning.

More decorating thrift plays out in garage sale bed frames and secondhand sofas and chairs. Dressed or re-covered in watercolor fabrics, these furnishings reflect what this house is all about: creating comfort for today without sacrificing timeworn charm.

FOCUSED ATTENTION
opposite **Open spaces call for well-placed details to ensure a pretty view when you're looking in from another room. In the kitchen, buttons detail the backs of stool slipcovers, weathered exterior siding clads half-walls, and linen draperies dress the window— creating engaging points of interest.**

TREASURE TROVE
above **A shelf full of seashells collected from travels and shelves loaded with books put a personal stamp on the living room. When displaying collections, group the items for impact. Spreading them throughout a home or even a room leads to a cluttered look.**

save the patina

Charm is the big selling point for vintage cottages, so try to preserve original finishes when you renovate. Embrace imperfections. Don't fret about dinged wood floors. Give them a good cleaning and leave them as they are. If something is really scuffed, put a rug on top. Decorating with pieces that have a similar aged look will tie things together. **Reuse and rethink.** Items salvaged from one project can be used for another. In this home, antique corbels detail the kitchen peninsula and exterior siding clads half-walls. **Swap in reproductions.** If something is just too far gone, mimic a vintage look. Subway tile, hexagonal flooring, apron-front and pedestal sinks, and schoolhouse lights say vintage even when they're new.

sweet dreams

ON THE WALL

above left A grouping of English china creates an artful display that mimics the shape of the bedroom dresser.

COLOR CONNECTION

left Patterned fabric is a great uniter, bringing continuity to a multicolor scheme. A chair slipcovered in taffy-color stripes ties together pastel furniture and accessories in the upstairs sitting area.

BATH REVIVAL

above Subway and mosaic tile give the new bathroom a fitting vintage look. An old claw-foot tub and a pedestal sink that were reglazed and fitted with old-style faucets enhance the look, while a table painted apple green lends function and fun.

SWEET AND SASSY

opposite Contrasts give a room energy. In the bedroom, a painting with vibrant colors cuts the sweetness of the floral bedding. Folding the floral comforter and letting the solid-color linens star also ensures that the room isn't overly sweet. Translucent glass lamps that resemble sea glass bring sleek style into a mix of furniture with fussier curves.

Try this!
Saw an old table
in half to use
as nightstands,
anchoring backs to
the wall.

BRIGHT SPOTS
White denim slipcovers and crisp white woodwork brighten this home's pale gray walls. Whitewashing gives the red brick fireplace a mellow appearance.

out of the shadows

Gray steps out as the surprising starting point color in this home. The key to shaking its drab reputation? Plenty of white and splashes of red.

It might not top the list of go-to colors, but gray has its place in cottage-style decorating. The timeless hue launched the scheme of this 1912 charmer. Far from being drab or stiff, the home is fresh and inviting, thanks to an abundance of white for brightness and splashes of red for warmth and energy.

The gray—ranging from light dove to charcoal—came with a big bonus: It's a neutral, so it's easy to change the look. Virtually any accent color works with the classic hue.

The home's fuss-free decorating formula plays out in other ways, too. Washable slipcovers and all-weather fabrics protect upholstery, while worn wood furniture and woven rugs stand up to heavy traffic. Open windows and Dutch doors let in fresh breezes year-round. And even when an overcast sky that mimics the gray hues inside looms, the cottage maintains its uplifting mood.

Try this!
Use marine paint on cabinets for a durable finish that resists moisture and salt air.

gray days
The in-between color of black and white, gray can put a fresh face on any room.

Be strategic. For walls, consider light gray as an alternative to white. It goes with everything, but it's not as stark. Unless you really want drama, save the charcoal hues for smaller surfaces; a little goes a long way.

Make it shine. Silvery accents—even small items such as chrome cabinet knobs and lamp bases—give a gray scheme subtle sparkle.

Let simplicity reign. You can't go wrong when you pair gray with white and then bring in one accent color for impact. With red, the scheme is timeless. With yellow, the look is modern.

Add light. Layered lighting sources keep a gray scheme from falling flat. Supplement overhead lighting with table lamps, floor lamps, and sconces.

THE LOWDOWN
The striped rug gives the kitchen an easy-to-change splash of red. The sink cabinet gains a furniture look with curved legs detailing the toe-kick area.

FADE AWAY
above left Charcoal and black soapstone for the countertops and backsplash tiles provides a seamless look.

ON THE BOARDWALK
above middle Black awnings and a gray roof set the home apart and hint at the interior scheme.

VARIETY SHOW
above right A mix of textures, in wicker chairs, the worn wood table, and woven blinds, brings cottage character to the dining room.

HERE TO STAY
right Fabrics—black-and-white ticking on the sofa and gray denim on the window seat cushions—set a timeless tone in the living room. Striped pillows chime in for more classic style.

out of the shadows

COMMON GROUND
The striped bedding and rug echo the pattern of the master bedroom's board-and-batten walls. Complementary quilts offer the flexibility to change the look.

SPACE EXPLORATION
above left A three-drawer dresser with a small mirror hung above makes functional use of a snug under-the-eaves space. The dresser and a trunk at the end of the bed (shown opposite) help compensate for skimpy closets. High-gloss paint on the antique dresser brightens the dim corner.

SITTING PRETTY
above right A cushy chair and ottoman turn a corner of the bedroom into an inviting reading nook. When carving out a bedroom sitting area, focus on the chair first; it won't get used if it's not comfy. To eke out extra chair space, trade a table-and-lamp combo for a floor lamp.

Washable slipcovers reflect easy-living cottage style. Remove them from the dryer when slightly damp so they're easier to put back on and have some give to readily conform to the furniture's shape.

FUN AND FRIENDLY
Cane inserts on cabinet doors provide earthy texture in this white kitchen. A glass star pendant and the original range are eye-catching features—one playful, the other nostalgic.

natural instinct

Embracing an indoor-outdoor connection, this laid-back family home seems bigger, looks brighter, and lives better—without an addition.

Clean and simple, with fun pieces that stand out: That's the strategy behind this snug 1,100-square-foot family home that gained a space and style boost inspired by nature. Curtain-free windows expand the horizon to visually stretch the small living room, dining area, and kitchen. White walls achieve a feeling of openness throughout the home and serve as blank canvases for layering in lighthearted accessories, including a shell chandelier that nods to the home's breezy coastal setting and driftwood used to decorate tabletops.

The biggest boost from nature, though, takes place beyond the home's four walls. A much-used covered patio with a sturdy old picnic table extends living and dining outdoors, giving the family a fresh-air retreat rain or shine.

natural instinct

LIGHT TOUCH
Lighting can make or break a room. In the dining area, a capiz shell chandelier reflects the home's near-the-beach location. Pushing the table up to a new built-in storage bench is a smart use of floor space.

Try this!
Stack vintage suitcases to use as an end table; the insides make great storage.

INSIDE OUT

above left **A countertop** that runs indoors and out is a fun and handy feature—just slide food and drinks through the open window to the patio. Its stainless steel stands up to spills and the weather and brings a sleek look to the classic kitchen. Small shelves flanking the window serve as platforms for plates when entertaining.

EXTEND THE VIEW

above right **If** privacy isn't an issue, let windows go bare to heighten the connection to the outdoors and allow more natural light inside. Here, the original 12-foot-wide window draws the eyes outside, making the small living room seem larger.

CASUAL DINING

right A picnic table adds a nostalgic touch on the renovated covered patio. Wicker chairs pulled up to the ends make the table seem more formal. Succulents trailing over the sides of a candelabra create a soft focal point overhead, while black pebbles detailing a concrete floor stained to look old create ground-level interest.

natural instinct

HARDWORKING BATH
Siding on walls gives the compact bath—gained by stealing space from the master bedroom—vintage character. Wall-mount faucets and open and closed storage in the vanity make efficient use of the tight space.

ON THE SIDE

below Smart furniture arrangements work wonders in a small house. In the boy's bedroom, a twin-size bed pushed parallel to the wall frees play space at the center of the room. With pillows against the wall, the bed resembles a daybed. For whimsical artwork, vintage sock monkeys climb aboard an oar.

SERENE SCENE

right The master bedroom achieves a cozy calmness with solid colors— soothing blue, sandy beige, and crisp white—in large expanses of fabric; pattern is restricted to easy-to-change pillows. Built-ins flanking the bed allow dresser-free storage, with a ledge for a few bedside necessities.

VISUAL TREATS

A woven trunk that looks
like an oversize picnic
basket and a shutter
propped by the door
reflect a penchant for
working salvaged pieces
into everyday decor.

full of character

Salvaged pieces and castoffs find new purpose in a home decorated to create a comfy, shabby-meets-elegant atmosphere.

Living in a new house doesn't mean forfeiting the charm of an old one. Take, for example, this modular home: Smartly outfitted with salvaged items, it has the charisma and character of a classic cottage. Century-old tin tiles cover ceilings, a salvaged mantel centers a statement-making vignette, and reclaimed doors, shutters, and windows propped against walls add an easy-to-move layer of personality.

To keep a decorating scheme that's built on salvaged and flea market pieces from looking more shabby than chic, follow a simple rule: Pair something old and rustic with something elegant. In this home, crystal chandeliers do the trick. Sparkling above rustic farm tables, slipcovered sofas, and a bed dressed in vintage linens, the chandeliers bring a hint of glamour into the charming mix.

SMALL WONDER

above Lots of white, including the paint on a wall-spanning cupboard, keeps the living area feeling open. A barn door set on two old sawhorses becomes a desk, while an antique Swedish clock and sheer curtains hanging from birch branches add whimsy.

VINTAGE FLAIR

left Vintage accessories—ironstone pitchers atop the refrigerator, canning jars on a window ledge, and French linens—tone down the newness of the kitchen. Cabinets are painted pale gray for warmth. In the dining area, an antique chandelier hangs above a farmhouse table.

Think beyond moldings and trim to give a home architectural interest. A salvaged mantel adds abundant character and becomes a statement piece that can be moved to a different room to change the look. White semigloss paint brings a slightly modern edge to the formerly pink mantel. Here and throughout the house, pale gray walls give white pieces depth.

full of character

LIGHT FARE

The dining room, which flows from the kitchen's eating area, has a keep-it-casual sensibility. Flea market bistro chairs scoot up to a farmhouse table painted glossy white for a crisp and clean look. Breezy sheers allow light to filter in. A zinc pitcher with a worn finish becomes sculpture, displayed on a table in front of the window.

full of character

WINDOW DRESSING
A 19th-century Spanish window from a schoolhouse becomes an intriguing backdrop for the 1920s French table used as a desk. An old shutter and hydrangeas in an antique apothecary jar add more interest.

SALVAGED BLISS

above right Get creative to give a bedroom character. Here, French barn doors become a grand headboard, and an old crate serves as a rustic nightstand. Antique tin tiles from a salvage yard cover the ceiling, making the room seem like it's part of an 1800s home. The showy crystal chandelier delightfully counters the room's rustic elements.

OUTDOOR LIVING

right An arbor lush with climbing roses is a sweet passageway to a stone patio. The painted dining table, rather than a standard patio table, makes the space seem like a furnished room. Wine barrels used as planters and a display of watering cans add charm.

touch of elegance

Cottage style dresses up beautifully. Bring out its sophisticated side with soft colors, well-chosen accessories, and pretty fabrics. These homes provide the inspiration.

GARDEN-INSPIRED
Roman shades with an embroidered lattice design complement the floral fabric used for pillows. Aqua accents, including the leather on the chairs, add a fresh, modern edge.

pattern play

Florals, lattice, ginghams, plaids—this home welcomes them all. The key to avoiding overload? Limiting the color scheme and changing up the scale.

When it comes to pattern, cottage style celebrates variety. A mix of prints—florals, checks, stripes—layers a space with personality and can enhance a home's architecture.

This home drew inspiration from a country inn, where florals, ginghams, and plaids called to mind a charming English cottage in the countryside. Greens and pinks keep the look classic, while touches of aqua freshen the scheme. The colors thread throughout rooms, providing a unifying theme and easy flow. In main rooms, such as the dining and living areas, pattern plays a bit role, appearing subtly in pillows and window treatments. In the master suite, it stars: A modern tulip print that complements apple-green walls launches spring-fresh style. Plaids and ginghams in greens, blues, and raspberry complete the look—one that's romantic and sophisticated without frills or fuss.

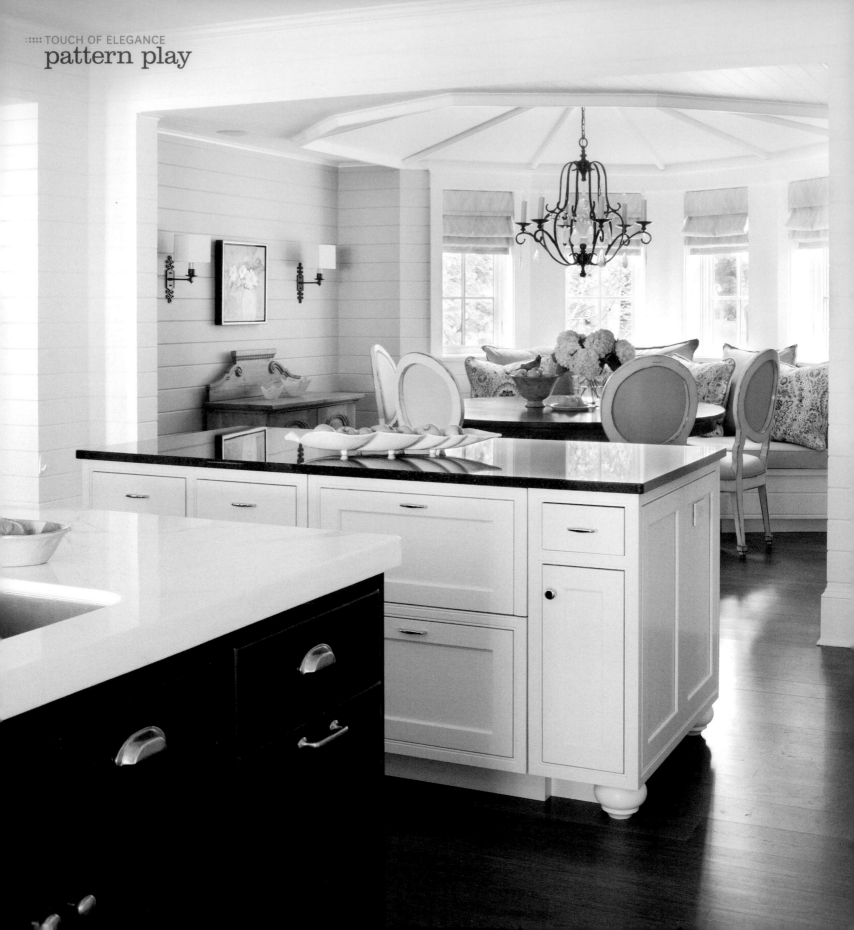

REVERSE ORDER

opposite **Mixing charcoal-gray and white cabinets gives the kitchen an unfitted look. Polished black granite on the white island provides a sleek, modern vibe—and reverses the color scheme of the gray cabinetry.**

THE BIG PICTURE

above **Despite its muted colors, the area rug boasts the dominant pattern in the living area. Bolder prints, such as the raspberry check and wide stripe, are reserved for small pillows so there's no competition. The pale aqua ceiling links to the color of the sofa and accessories.**

making pattern work

Adding pattern is an easy way to pull together a color scheme. Consider these tips. Establish order. Select fabrics first, then match paint colors to your choices. For a no-fail scheme, use two patterns in the same colors. Vary the scale. Set the palette with a large-scale pattern, then support it with solids and smaller-scale prints. Add a flower or two. Cottage schemes often reflect gardens, so floral fabrics are a natural. Splurge and save. If you fall in love with a pricey fabric, use it for an accent pillow or a table runner. You'll get impact without the expense.

Try this!
Use a side table as a nightstand to visually balance a tall headboard or high bed.

SPRING FRESH

A chenille headboard commands attention in the master bedroom, its apple-green hue blending with the walls and the silk plaid used for the bed skirt. The coverlet's scalloped edge plays off the curves of the headboard. A secondary color in the embroidered tulip fabric inspired the pale aqua accents, including the lattice-motif rug, which adds a big dose of pattern.

LUSH LAYERS
Stationary curtain panels frame the dressing table, setting it off as a focal point. A wide band of aqua-and-white gingham provides visual relief from the table's larger-scale tulip fabric.

BALANCED OUT
above left When mixing patterns, vary the scales. Here, a large-scale plaid silk covering the club chair tames the pattern mix. An aqua velvet chaise longue grounds the setting.

SWEET SURPRISE
above middle Raspberry-painted walls and a pretty chandelier ensure that the master bedroom closet is a vibrant space.

UNITED FRONT
above right A lattice-inspired design on cabinet doors visually links the master bath to the bedroom rug. Marble countertops keep the space light and airy.

FABRIC SOFTENERS
right With plaid fabric shirred on its doors, an armoire exudes cottage charm. The plaid repeats as trim on the chair cushion and valance for continuity and softness.

OPPOSITES ATTRACT
A chandelier with beads draped from a metal form and classic-looking chairs covered in rattan reflect this home's play on rustic and elegant.

country chic

Beads and crystals, burlap and iron: They're part of the mix in this small farmhouse —and they're what give it its upscale-meets-rustic intrigue.

How do you square a desire for sophistication when your reality is a small, no-frills home? It's all in the details. In this 1,750-square foot farmhouse, elegance wraps itself in an appropriately rustic package. Hardware-store rope suspends pendants detailed with sparkling crystals, and basic pine beams from a lumberyard accent ceilings.

The renovated home's fancy-meets-humble detailing takes its style cue from old French farmhouses. A hammer and chisel were all it took to distress new pine beams and give them the illusion of age. In the kitchen, light and dark finishes make stock cabinetry look more interesting. Fleur-de-lis hardware dresses up timeworn doors. The result is a home that is sophisticated, livable, and totally appropriate for its country setting.

UNFITTED CHARM

opposite To express rustic style using modern materials, mix things up. In this kitchen, stock cabinetry receives a custom look with a blend of dark and light finishes and solid and glass-front doors. Reproduction French chandeliers look rustically elegant suspended from hardware-store rope.

RELAXED LIVING

above A slipcovered sofa with an attached chaise longue keeps the living room on the casual side. Here, as in other rooms, the interest is overhead. Burlap flows over an antique wire fixture, displaying a sassy ruffle. Pine beams with custom-designed braces add architectural interest.

Light fixtures are jewelry for a home. An interesting pendant or chandelier boosts a room's sophistication and character. Sconces serve as wall art.

Earthy colors and natural finishes reflect the home's surroundings.

LOCAL COLOR
above The renovated 1880s home nestles into its wooded setting with chocolate-brown siding and a bright green door.

MODERN TWIST
right An open shower detailed with pebbles, travertine, and a raised edge veers the bathroom toward contemporary. Because the stone is rustic, the look works with other rooms.

COZY ALCOVE
below right With an arched ceiling and a niche for books, the window seat alcove in the guest bedroom seems almost like a room of its own. New hardware with a fleur-de-lis at each end brings a touch of style to timeworn doors.

SPACE SMARTS
far right Windows in the master bedroom function as a headboard, drawing the eyes outside. The box spring rests on the floor so the low ceiling seems higher.

dress up the deck

Pull elements of French style outdoors to give a patio or deck a sophisticated look.

Skip the patio set. Rusted metal pieces hint at country French style. Use an old iron table with ornate detailing. Pull up a bench or wicker chairs. A bistro table is a stylish option for a small space.

Borrow from indoors. Look for accessories that can live outdoors, such as a copper pot, an old pitcher, a wire basket, or bottles. Use the vessels for flowers or just as pretty accessories.

Soften with fabrics. A burlap runner on a table or pillows in chairs add homey comfort.

Add some life. Pots of herbs, such as rosemary and basil, add French flair and also can be used in cooking. Ivy creeping up a trellis from a stone planter creates a lush backdrop.

OUTDOOR ELEGANCE
A copper-top iron table outfitted with towering candelabra brings French-inspired style to the deck.

SUBTLE NUANCES
A delicate French love seat and a shapely sofa found abroad lend a European air to the living room, while nesting tables relax the effect.

warming trend

By translating a European design aesthetic, this small cottage gains a cozy, upscale look. More than sophisticated, it's practical, too.

For a change of pace from all-American whites, give cottage style a Belgian twist. The European design philosophy built around the idea of simple luxury could be considered cottage's mysterious cousin. Subdued colors— in this Cape Cod-style home, it's a stone palette of grays and browns—unfold for a somewhat moody sensibility that cocoons rooms in comfort.

Like classic cottage, the Belgian look welcomes contradictions. Here, furnishings run the gamut—a $25 secondhand sofa, a French love seat, and a midcentury modern dining table, for example. Fabrics reveal more contrasts. In the living room, humble burlap customizes striped velvet draperies—a trick that makes the off-the-rack velvet treatments fuller and more luxurious. That unexpected pairing gets to the heart of Belgian style: It might take on airs of richness, but it's never pretentious.

warming trend

defining belgian

An authentic Belgian look comprises a mix of elements. Bring in a few or all.

Start with the palette. Subdued color is a signature. Repeat shades of grays and earth tones to create a moody effect.

Look up. Hang oversize lanterns and chandeliers. If rooms are small, choose a more appropriate scale and delicate fixtures. A glass lantern, for example, won't take up much visual space.

Lighten the tone. Raw, limed, or bleached wood furniture is the norm. Clean-lined modern or industrial pieces are typically in the mix, too.

Add contrast. Play the high-low game by pairing velvet with burlap, hemp, or linen. With furniture and accessories, blend pedigreed pieces with flea market finds.

GROUP THERAPY
Displayed together on shelves in the breakfast nook, flower paintings discovered at flea markets make an impact. Casually propped, they look less formal.

CREATIVE TWIST

above left Slipcovered Parsons chairs get a kick with backs covered in antique feed sacks stamped with the original owner's crest. Ready-to-assemble bookcases flanking the window mimic the look of built-ins.

WELL-EDITED

above middle Objects with nature themes and similar colors create an eye-pleasing display on a hutch.

GRAPHIC FLAIR

above right The mood lifts in the bedroom, where wide horizontal stripes on walls modernize the classic scheme. For a similar subtle effect, choose three shades from the same paint card.

SEAT SWAP

right Benches can be the saving grace in a small dining room, taking up less space and seating more people than chairs. Here, slipcovered storage benches tuck under an antique picnic-style table.

ADDED INTEREST
A distressed birdbath filled with moss balls eases the formality of the entry. Weathered paneling retrofitted with a mirror mimics the look of a trumeau.

fluent in french

Muted colors, subtle textures, and old-world finishes inspired by European design sensibilities foster an air of low-key elegance.

The love affair with French style continues. In the past, warm reds and golden yellows offered a colorful palette for the Provence look. Today, muted hues create soothing and interchangeable backdrops for a more sophisticated take on country French style.

This 1930s home keeps the palette airy with slipcovers, fabrics, and walls in creams, grays, and browns. Woven natural-fiber rugs, limestone tile, and hardwood flooring pair with beaded-board paneling and patinaed furnishings for tactile texture that enhances the subdued scheme. Found accessories create a character-rich atmosphere that honors the French tradition of living with unusual pieces. But rather than cover every surface as in the past, today's one-of-a-kind finds are more restrained to reflect a calling for simplicity and uncomplicated living.

ABOVE BOARD

opposite A ceiling holds decorating opportunity; think of it as a room's fifth wall. In the family room, cypress boards cladding the tray ceiling were treated and stained to mimic salvaged barnwood. The shapely chandelier crafted from antique wine barrels inspired the look.

EASY LIVING

above Easy-wash unsealed outdoor pavers set a neutral palette in a pass-through space used as a sitting room. Gray grout between the pavers hides dirt and works with the home's neutral scheme. The draperies, pillows, coffee table, light fixtures, and walls echo the tiles' golden hues.

bringing neutrals to life

Limiting walls and foundation pieces to muted hues creates a sophisticated look. If you want to add color, ease it in so you maintain the mood. Go natural. Place blooming plants and fresh-cut flowers throughout the house. Natural-color blooms, such as limy green hydrangeas or bells of Ireland, add a burst of color while enhancing the scheme. Fade away. When adding pattern, use antique floral prints or those with a faded look to give a soft touch of color. Look at the back side of fabrics and rugs, too; sometimes the back is more interesting and color-appropriate than the front. Add pillows. Incorporate patterned pillows to lend low-commitment visual texture to a room.

fluent in french

BOLD STATEMENT
The dining room deviates slightly from the home's neutral scheme with graphic green-and-white curtains. The damask-inspired pattern complements a mix of reproduction and antique furnishings, including a pair of 200-year-old doors and a candle-powered chandelier that casts a warm glow on the room.

OPEN AND CLOSE
Drapery panels dressing the French doors allow the master bedroom to be closed off from the sitting room—a simple way to gain privacy without shrouding the glass with fabric shirred on a rod.

RESTFUL PALETTE

below Classic toile, rendered in shades of soft brown and cream, strikes a masculine note in the master bedroom while playing to the home's theme of timelessness. Matelassé linens and a whitewashed nightstand and caned bed provide a snowy yet textural backdrop for the toile pillows. A sconce offers bedside lighting without a lamp taking space on the petite nightstand.

TIME TO SHINE

right A bit of sparkle—in brass, chrome, or mirrored surfaces—is important in every room, especially one with an earthy, muted scheme that needs elements to sharpen the focus. Here, an architectural salvage lamp and framed art share similar golden tones, brightening the carved desk and chair.

welcoming retreats

Small cottages built as getaways started
the trend toward living with a relaxed style
year-round. That easygoing attitude prevails
in these vacation-minded homes.

SEA

PERKY COMEBACK
Margarita-green paint updates the look of an old metal glider—which in turn jazzes up a classic white wicker grouping on the screen porch.

back in time

The living is easy in this retro-cool beach cottage. Splashed with juicy color and infused with a hint of 1950s kitsch, it beckons good times indoors and out.

Owning a summer home is almost a license to have fun. It offers a chance to loosen up, try something different, and play with color. This beach retreat embraces the idea with a retro design that takes its cues from pastel-color cottages from the 1940s and '50s.

Think funky—and even a little junky—to create a vintage coastal look. Shop estate sales, flea markets, and online auction sites for furniture and accessories. Fabrics, such as bark-cloth curtains and chenille bedspreads, set a retro vibe, too.

In this cottage, white walls serve as a clean base for colorful vintage gems and playful accessories, including swimwear framed and hung as art. Outside, full-on color—the minty-green exterior and flamingo-pink screen door—adds '50s-inspired curb appeal that inspires passersby to remember when.

CLUTTER BUSTERS

left A beach house calls for an entry that stylishly organizes summertime essentials. An old hall tree juiced up with turquoise paint offers grab-and-go ease for hats, sunglasses, and more. Metal buckets and bins that corral beach towels and flip-flops can be easily hosed down outside. Displayed in frames, swimwear makes fun and affordable art.

COLORFUL PRESENCE

below Mint-green paint on the exterior, a pink door, and a white picket fence take the 1940s cottage back to its former glory.

SECONDHAND STYLE

bottom An old cast-iron kitchen sink and horizontal-plank walls ensure the updated kitchen has an old-school look. Vintage plates make pretty use of often-empty space above doors.

FIFTIES FLASHBACK
An assemblage of vintage
pieces—including lamps
and rattan chairs—
decorates the living
room. Shutters, sharing
the same warm wood
tone as the chairs and
wicker trunk, are
a classic way to add
cottage appeal.

WORKING IT

above left A rotary phone, typewriter, and old-fashioned fan set a period-appropriate mood. On the wall, framed book jackets create colorful and affordable art. Comb through bins at used bookstores for summer-theme titles with graphic cover illustrations.

BATHROOM BEAUTY

above right Bathrooms have as much decorating potential as any other room in the house. Here, powder blue walls show off crisp white storage cubbies filled with little pretties, such as shells and bottles. The outdoor planter next to the refurbished claw-foot tub could be used to hold rolled-up towels or a basket of toiletries.

ON DISPLAY

opposite Vintage castoffs get new life as character-rich accessories in the bedroom. An enamelware pan serves as a vase, and a cosmetic case pulls duty as a nightstand drawer, providing storage for tissues and other items.

Try this!
Wall-mount
swing-arm lamps
free up table space
and let you direct
task lighting.

evoke an era

Take a home back in time with a few signature items—and comforting sounds.

Hang a new door. A screen door adds more than vintage charm. The sound of its closing or creaking takes many people back to their childhood. Wooden doors say old school. Aluminum ones— especially in a color such as pink—say retro.

Head outside. Spending time on the porch or in the backyard was big in the '50s—as was colorful metal furniture. Look for vintage gliders and shell-back chairs at antiques stores and flea markets. Use a wire brush to remove rust, then paint the piece a bright color. Or go with a reproduction.

Cool off. The whir of a fan calls to mind hot summer days before air-conditioning. If the wiring isn't up to snuff, simply use a vintage fan as an accessory.

RELAXED ATTITUDE
Aqua garden stools, a faux-coral lamp with sea horse pulls, coral-pattern fabrics, and a koi painting give the living room sophisticated island style.

carefree spirit

Watery hues and beachy accessories give this home an easygoing quality.
It's a breezy style you can re-create even if there's no coastline outside your door.

When you're on island time, the pace slows, worries fade, and relaxation rises to the top of the agenda. This home slips into that carefree mode with a decorating scheme that embraces its island setting without going overboard.

Renovated to resemble an old beach cottage, the 1980s home captivates with white beaded board covering walls and ceilings. Pale aquas and sea-glass hues that play off the white backdrops add a breezy quality, while hits of red energize. Sofas, chairs, and chaise longues in relaxed fabrics such as cottons and linens have a sink-into-it comfort.

For all the relaxation, though, there's a playfulness to the decor. Knobs shaped like coral detail kitchen cabinets. Elsewhere, shells and faux coral appear on lamps and tables. But the decor is more sophisticated than themey—yet still appropriately laid-back, just as an island home should be.

EVOKE A FEEL
The dining room incorporates textures that lend a casual look. A Russian oak table lightened with a wash, a seagrass rug, and linen slipcovers have a beachy feel. The focal-point cabinet is outfitted with doors made from antique windows.

DEFINING DETAILS
above Details distinguish the kitchen, where rustic corbels on the island add character and stools are designed after old schoolhouse chairs. Pendants with an antiqued brass finish ensure the room doesn't look too sleek and modern; the color links to the copper screen in the pantry door (right).

CORAL CONNECTION
right Coral knobs bring the sea's ambience inside—and lend a playful side to the beaded-board cabinet doors. The wooden art piece is an old tabletop, hand-painted with a coral motif.

BEDROOM BLISS

opposite This bedroom reflects the home's island setting without being overtly theme-ish. A drum-style accent table shimmers with capiz shell covering, and an old jar filled with shells becomes a lamp. The headboard was designed to recall gingerbread porch rails and pickets.

AWASH IN STYLE

above left A console-style sink gives the bath a furnished look. A distressed stand-alone cabinet provides storage—and also adds character.

STEPPING BACK

above right A freestanding tub with vintage styling becomes an elegant centerpiece in the bath. Hexagonal tiles on the floor and subway tiles on walls add more vintage-inspired charm.

SITTING PRETTY

right Comfortable fabrics go hand-in-hand with a casual seaside retreat. In the master bedroom, chaise longues covered in cotton slipcovers provide soft spots to relax. Their sea-glass color nods to the room's ocean views. Sheer curtains keep the palette crisp and clean.

FRESH-AIR RESPITE
Sleeping porches still
have their place in
today's cottages, even if
it's just for afternoon
naps. Mattresses encased
in durable custom-quilted
fabric enhance the
nostalgic appeal of this
in-the-treetops porch.

sense of place

This cozy escape embraces its woodsy setting with earthy colors and twiggy accents while offering fresh ideas on what a cabin can be.

Listen to your surroundings. That's a lesson interior designers take to heart, and it's a good motivator whenever you're stuck in a decorating rut. Simply look out the windows, and let nature be your guide. Blue waters and sandy beaches? Rugged mountains and thick woods? Rolling hills and green valleys? Whatever you see can launch a look that heightens the indoor-outdoor connection, making a getaway more special.

In this 1901 cedar-shake home, an earthy palette of brown and green with hints of aqua plays off the woodsy location, where blue sky peeks between trees. Rustic accents, including branches formed into furniture and supports for kitchen shelves, further distinguish the indoor-outdoor connection. But the look is far from cabin-in-the-woods cliché. Graphic fabrics with motifs such as deer and leaves are as fresh-looking as the air is invigorating.

NATURAL CHARM
Birch chairs and a twig chandelier bring the woodsy look to the dining room. Fabric on the armchairs and draperies features an artful interpretation of leaves and deer, injecting pastoral subject matter with modern attitude. The inside of the hutch was painted a contrasting cream so majolica-style pottery stands out—an easy makeover for any cabinet or bookcase.

Try this!
Display collections in a glass case or under a cloche to make them look more special.

BRIGHTENED UP

A coffee table topped with wood planks showing their age creates a conversation-starting focal point in the walk-out lower-level family room, where apple green walls lift the mood. A space-defining woven rug tops durable, moisture-resistant tile, a practical option in a lower-level space. The area near the back door functions as a mudroom, with baskets holding outdoor gear.

BRANCHING OUT
top left Birch limbs cleverly support kitchen shelves, a reminder of the home's wooded location.

PRETTY IMPOSTOR
top middle Gain the comfy, stay-awhile appeal of a built-in banquette with a table and settee. In this eating area, an upholstered bench that looks like an oversize wing chair cozies up to an antique table.

HOMESPUN CHARM
top right Banks of cabinetry can make a kitchen look hard and cold. This space shows a softer side with cabinets skirted with checked fabric. Also used for stools, the fabric sets a casual cottage tone.

INTO THE WOODS
bottom left and *bottom right* The custom coffee table and end tables on the porch were made to look as though twigs had been gathered from the woods and bundled together.

Weave the same colors throughout a home, including outdoor spaces, for easy flow. For variety, change the distribution; a color that stars in one room becomes an accent in the next.

MIXED MASTERY
Refined pieces—the bed, upholstered bench, and bedside desk—impart elegant style in the master bedroom. Still, the space continues the home's rustic character with exposed ceiling beams, walls clad in pine beaded board, a twig sconce, and a table lamp with a trunklike base.

SHADES OF SUMMER
Vintage canning jars and tableware inspired the blue hues that thread throughout this lightened-up retreat.

BEACH

casual grace

Beach retreats aren't all play and no sophistication. This whitewashed getaway strikes a balance so it's a little bit dressy yet plenty carefree.

Easy living is a given with a beach retreat. But that doesn't mean you can't sprinkle a little sophistication into the mix. A case in point is this vintage cottage. With wicker furniture and seagrass floor coverings, the decor sticks to script in terms of carefree beach style. The difference is in the layers that hint at formality. The wicker furniture is plumped with pillows, some bearing classic monograms. Nailhead trim details club chairs and an oversize ottoman with turned legs, lending traditional flair. Gingham draperies puddle on the floor, imparting a dressy look and also softening plantation shutters. In a bedroom, there's even a touch of toile for French-inspired class.

Still, with a backdrop of whitewashed knotty pine walls, the home retains the easygoing spirit a beach retreat needs. The lesson? A casual getaway can be both dressed up and relaxed.

Try this!
Use indoor-outdoor fabrics when you need fade resistance and durability.

A LITTLE WHIMSY
opposite Not the usual cottage fare, a giraffe-print ottoman adds a fun surprise in the living room. A striped rug layered atop the seagrass flooring brings in more pattern and also defines the sitting area.

FRAME THE VIEW
top right Draperies soften the transition between two living areas. The panels hang on a rod across the doorway so the rooms can be closed off for privacy; for a purely decorative look, hang panels from hooks.

QUICK CHANGE
middle right Removing doors from upper cabinets is an easy way to mimic the look of open shelving common to old kitchens. In this kitchen, the whitewashed pine cabinets display a vintage ironstone collection and everyday dishes—all white for a unified look.

OUTDOOR LIVING
bottom right A new outdoor living space surfaced with pea gravel and concrete slabs fronts the quaint cottage. The space features a seating area with teak love seats and chairs and lush plantings for softness and privacy.

consider every surface

Walls, floors, ceilings—they're important players in cottage style. Think about the backdrops before you bring in furniture. Start with a classic. Beaded board creates cottage style faster than any other element. Sheets of paneling with tongue-and-groove edges cost less and are easier to install than traditional wood strips. Bare it all. Hardwood floors offer an easy-care surface that looks good with soft fabrics and subdued color schemes. For a crisper look, paint floors white and seal with clear polyurethane. Lighten up. If knotty pine makes your home seem more cabin than cottage, whitewash it. Brush on a glaze with white paint mixed in, or hire a professional to pickle the walls for you.

TOILE DELIGHT

right **A little bit of pattern works wonders in any room. Here, oversize toile pillows dressing the antique bed lend a dash of French elegance and ensure that the simply decorated bedroom isn't a sea of solids. With its pastoral scenes, toile lends itself to bedrooms and other spaces where relaxation is the goal.**

FRESH TAKE

opposite top **Teal accents bring refreshing ocean color into the master bedroom while still working with the living room's calmer shade of blue. Surrounded by white, the lively accent color doesn't overwhelm.**

SPA INSPIRATION

opposite bottom **Floor-to-ceiling tile can make a small bath look larger by eliminating visual stops and starts. In this streamlined bath, aqua tiles and white accessories, including fluffy towels, set a soothing, spa-like atmosphere. The dresser-style sink vanity offsets the room's sleekness.**

special spaces

Homes today have to handle a lot. We crave places to relax as much as spots to craft, compute, or simply drop things off. Stylish and adaptable, these spaces answer the call.

porches | looks we love

Ahh...the porch. It might well be the best-loved feature of any cottage. And it's a delight to decorate. Bring on the wicker, hang a swing, or drape it with curtains—just make it yours.

RENEW YOURSELF

above left **Nothing says old-fashioned comfort more than a swing— something people young and old gravitate to. (A glider offers a similar lulling motion.) Another smart addition: a ceiling fan. Ceiling fans make balmy evenings bearable, and the circulating air helps keep bugs away.**

BREEZY ATTITUDE

above right **All-weather curtain panels softly divide this long porch into multiple rooms, offering a bit of shelter and privacy. Sturdy and weather-resistant galvanized pipe suspends the grommeted panels. For streetside privacy, hang panels along the front of the porch.**

RUSTIC RELAXATION

opposite left **With a big stone fireplace and stone floor, this porch seems one with the outdoors. The rustic touches, though, don't detract from the space's elegant looks. A sparkling chandelier and pretty fabrics add softness. A pewter deer head hanging near the fireplace provides whimsy.**

SKY HIGH

opposite right **From pale powder to robin's egg, blue ceilings are making a comeback for their classic look and ability to visually lift a covered space skyward. Here, the painted ceiling and bouquet of lilacs add vintage flair, while stackable plastic chairs instead of wicker lend a modern edge.**

weather the elements

Keep your porch looking good longer by choosing items designed for outdoor use. Use all-weather fabrics. Outdoor fabrics resist fading from sunlight and moisture from rain. Today's wide selection offers something in every style and color palette. Be smart about paint. A good-quality exterior-grade paint is a smart investment because it's formulated to withstand harsh elements. Oil-base paints that are generally used for floors provide a durable, shiny finish that adds extra glow. With white paint and white wicker, the look is crisp, clean cottage. Size up the fan. Choose a ceiling fan that's appropriate for the space. Some fans are wet-rated for open areas, some are damp-rated for covered areas, and others are designed to resist rust in salt-prone ocean locations; never hang an indoor ceiling fan outside. For vintage style, look for a fan with an aged finish. For tropical flair or to complement wicker furniture, choose a fan with woven blades.

Whether you have a small nook or a grand wraparound, make the most of your porch with these ideas for comfy arrangements and clever accents.

PRETTY, PLEASE

For all-day lingering, treat your porch as an outdoor living room. Here, a washable cotton striped rug defines the seating area. Comfy furnishings—with pillow shams doubling as pretty covers for plain cushions—are positioned for chatting or curling up with a book. Traditional wicker gives the porch a quintessential summer look. For a more durable option, use all-weather wicker made of resin.

SWEET SPOT

left When hosting an outdoor gathering, get creative with the presentation. Designate a table for snacks and beverages, and add linens in your porch's color scheme. Elevate a lemonade dispenser on a cake stand or in a footed bowl to become a focal point and make pouring easy. Filling a hurricane with lemons or other citrus fruit is an easy way to add a pop of color. A paper parasol shields this display from the sun.

STYLISHLY SHADED

above left Floral fabric panels made from outdoor fabric shade the seating area and create a pretty backdrop. To make, back patterned fabric with a second fabric layer for stability; add grommets at the top, and hang panels from cup hooks. Clip weights to the panel bottoms to prevent them from blowing. Accentuate the look with low-cost details, such as a large paper lantern that creates the effect of a pendant light.

FLOWER POWER

above right Think beyond potted containers to freshen up a porch. Just as indoors, fresh flowers on a coffee table can lift spirits. Canning jars used as vases keep things casual—plus, there's no worry about bringing a precious breakable outside. For impact, group three or six jars on a colorful serving tray. Display just one or two blooms in each jar to keep the display carefree.

GARDEN PARTY

above left **Heighten the pleasure of outdoor entertaining with a well-dressed table. Set the scene with a floral all-weather tablecloth that echoes the outdoors. Paper parasols in pastels create an inexpensive casual "chandelier," suspended with fishing line. A mix of flea market chairs adds a laid-back cottage feel; slipcovers made of outdoor fabric dress up host chairs.**

SIMPLE CENTERPIECE

above right **For an easy table decoration, arrange potted succulents or herbs under glass cloches and intersperse them with single stems of flowers in bottles. For a soft effect, wrap the succulent pots with fabric or a cloth napkin and tie with twine.**

BETTER TOGETHER

opposite **When separating a porch into different sitting areas, treat each space as its own room. To make a lone bench feel sheltered and cozy, add a tall backdrop, such as a folding screen or room divider. Here, hinged-together flea-market shutters do the trick. A climbing plant for softness and color and a petite accent table complete the look.**

A prettily decorated porch is a breath of fresh air, beckoning you to step outside to savor simpler times and friendly conversations.

porches | before & after

1 Furniture and pillows make this a place worthy of hanging out.

2 A new door better suited to the home's architecture makes a good first impression.

3 A new floor and ceiling fan update the look.

A neglected porch doesn't do much for a home's curb appeal. Give it a little TLC, though, and it's a totally different story.

BEFORE
3 common flaws

1 What could be extra living space is a barren tract of pine.

2 No curb appeal—right down to the door that doesn't mesh with the bungalow's style.

3 The space is beginning to show its age—some 80 years.

NATURAL FIT

opposite With a mix of earthy fabrics that complement the bungalow's reddish bricks, the formerly stark porch is now warm and inviting. Containers of flowers soften the background and form a simple privacy screen.

TRANSFORMED TUB

top A metal washtub serves as an oversize planter. Brush on a stain-inhibiting primer, and paint the tub with exterior-grade paint. Use a stencil for the design, and protect it with clear spray sealant.

SOFT LANDING

middle left A cushion and pillows plump up comfort on the swing. For seasonal variety, swap patterned pillows—leaves for fall, a sun for summer.

SURPRISE INSIDE

middle right The top of the coffee table lifts to reveal its clever secret: it's also a beverage cooler, with galvanized washtubs resting on a plywood base. In lieu of beverages, the tubs can store pillows or outdoor gear.

WELCOMING HOME

bottom left Colorful mum-filled pots line the steps and draw the eye to the new cherry door. Ipe wood planks update the floor.

DOOR MONOGRAM

bottom right A monogram-inspired door hanger made from dowels is a nifty changeup from a wreath. Saw different diameter wood dowels into various lengths. Glue the dowel pieces to plywood cut in a letter shape. (Enlarge a computer-printed letter to use as a template.) Clear polyurethane spray protects the wood.

Try this!
To give a large arrangement needed height, use ornamental grass.

drop zones | looks we love

So much stuff, so little space. Instead of letting the influx of mail, backpacks, shoes—you name it—take over, designate a home for it. As these spaces show, drop zones have never looked better.

ORGANIZED ENTRY

above left **In a home without a mudroom, an entry hall has to handle a lot—so make it look good while it works hard. Here, a cushioned bench provides a place to put on shoes; baskets for sports gear and more tuck below. A petite table with small bowls and a bin becomes a drop spot for mail and keys. A coppery boot tray (much prettier than a plastic version) ensures that shoes don't pile on the floor.**

PACK AND WRAP

above right **Drop zones can be carved from unlikely spaces, such as this basement hallway set up as a mailing and wrapping station. Two steel worktops and shelves attach to a rail-style shelving system. An old postal meter holds a planter filled with shipping labels, and another planter contains ribbons threaded through mesh shelves. A vintage yardstick glued to a shelf front is always ready for a quick measurement.**

SCHOOL DAYS

opposite left **Create the ultimate drop zone with locker-inspired cubbies in a hall or garage entrance to your house. This freestanding unit gives a 6-foot-wide nook the function of a mudroom; look for cubbies in various sizes to fit your space. Wallpapered backs add dimension and a custom look. Striped bins have monogrammed labels—one for each family member.**

WORK CORNER

opposite right **A bold checkerboard design ensures that this tool landing spot brightens a corner of a garage or basement. Prime pegboard, paint it white, then mask off squares and paint them a bright color; it's best to have the pegboard lying flat to avoid drips. A potting bench takes the place of a standard tool bench; a kitchen island would work, too. Vintage baskets and bins provide character-rich storage.**

discover potential drop zones

You know the saying—a place for everything, and everything in its place. If you're short on space, consider nontraditional areas as your little landing spots. Rethink the front entry. Something as simple as a bookcase outfitted with baskets can give an entry hall new function. For bigger impact, remove the door from the coat closet and add shelves to emulate a built-in. Go low. Enlist the landing space at the bottom of the basement stairs as a pantry. Store overflow items, such as rolls of paper towels or small appliances that aren't often used, on a freestanding shelving unit. To hide the utility, drape it with fabric; if it's a console, skirt it. Consider the garage. If you have an attached garage that leads directly into your house—no little buffer in between—set up a mudroom in the garage. Hang shelves next to the door, and outfit them with baskets. Attach a decorative rail to the wall, and add hooks for coats. To dress up the space more, clad lower walls near the door with easy-to-wash panels that look like beaded board.

drop zones | get organized

Built-ins clad with beaded board and cabinetry with a few fun touches bring loads of functionality into this space—a garage entrance into the home.

STORAGE GALORE

The smart-looking built-in incorporates storage, seating, and hanging space. Wicker baskets add texture and a streamlined look; library-style holders on the shelf fronts identify the contents. Pillows form an easy-to-change seat cushion. Below the bench, a low shelf keeps dirty shoes off the floor. Beaded board echoes the style of the 1950s home, and chunky trim at eye level makes a handy spot for coat hooks.

OPEN AND CLOSED

above left **Whenever possible, incorporate** both open and closed storage into a room. You'll be able to close off things you simply don't want visible, yet still have areas that allow easy access. Here, upper cabinets serve as a pantry for canned goods, and lower shelves hold lined baskets for collecting dirty laundry. A walnut countertop visually warms the room.

PET PROJECT

above right **A paw print cutout on the door marks** the cabinet that houses the dog's retreat, outfitted with a cushion for napping. Below the cabinet, a drawer pulls out to reveal food and water bowls. A cabinet to the left of the kennel stores pet food.

ARTFULLY SAID

right **Every space benefits** from a little whimsy. Mismatched decorative letters accumulated from flea markets and garage sales spell an appropriate "Wash Dry" message on the laundry side of the room. A rod above the sink is handy for hanging clothes to dry or for family members to pick up on their way inside.

Remember when homes didn't have to be offices, too? There's no getting around that today. Get creative to squeeze in space for the computer—and all that comes with it—without sacrificing style.

BIG ON STYLE

above left **Having a home office doesn't require giving up an entire room. Here, a petite desk, positioned perpendicular to a wall in a living room, takes up just a sliver of space. The desk resembles a table (and can be used as a buffet). A wicker chair, vintage baskets, and a table lamp also have a look that says "home" more than "office.".**

COLOR CODED

above right **This living room pulls duty as an office, but with a repeating red-and-white scheme, the office and living areas blend. A white cotton skirt attached with hook-and-loop tape softens the wall-spanning desktop and hides supplies and computer equipment on pullout shelves. Simple shelves above store office essentials and display decorative items.**

TUCKED IN

opposite left **A between-the-studs hallway work space functions as a compact office without taking up living space. The desktop and drawers mimic the look of a traditional desk. Built slightly higher (at counter height), the desk can be used as a stand-up space for quickly checking e-mail messages on a laptop or writing checks.**

PRODUCTIVE PORCH

opposite right **A tiny enclosed porch becomes a hardworking office. To eke out as much storage as possible but still keep the space looking good, a skirt conceals the printer and file boxes. With no room for a cabinet, clipboards hang on the wall to provide a filing system to organize bills and documents.**

get down to business

Are you ready to carve out a home office—whether it's a nook or a room? Consider these work-smart options. Store in style. Skirted desktops do more than add a soft look and cottage charm—they hide a bevy of computer-related equipment. For on-the-shelf storage, scour flea markets for old picnic baskets or lunch boxes. Light it right. Good lighting is key to any work area. Save desktop space by flanking the desk with sconces or pendants. If you have enough room, a floor lamp works, too. Stay on top of clutter. Designate a vintage wire basket or a serving tray as your in-box. A cork or magnet board is an office essential; pretty one up by putting it in a vintage frame. Or paint a section of a wall with chalkboard paint to create a custom message center.

With paint, accessories, and hardworking furniture, a work space that looked like an afterthought is now pretty and productive.

BEFORE
3 common flaws

1 No clear definition. Is it an office? Sewing room? Dumping ground?

2 Folding tables for a desk, a kitchen chair, and little storage diminish productivity.

3 With bland makeshift furnishings, there is no sense of style.

3 fabulous fixes

1 A new desk, chair, and cabinet define the room's main role: office.

2 The L-shape desk offers lots of work space—and still allows room for the sewing machine.

3 Spring-green walls and pretty fabrics add homey comfort.

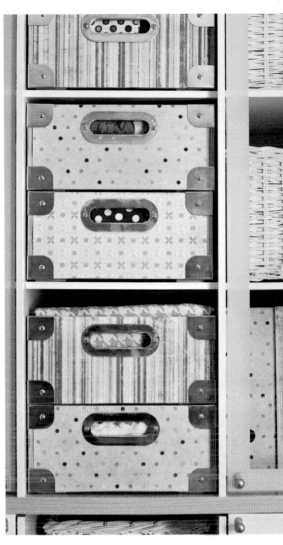

EFFICIENCY PLUS

left **An L-shape desk provides lots of room for spreading out, and inexpensive assemble-yourself cabinets offer storage that efficiently uses vertical space. The new office also scores big on style. A runner dresses up the desktop, and a slipcover makes a basic office chair on rollers look less businesslike.**

IN ORDER

top **Labels ensure that no time is wasted trying to remember what's inside each drawer. Get a similar look by stenciling drawer fronts, using adhesive letters, or installing library-style label holders designed for shelves.**

READY SUPPLIES

above left **Pencil cups and other desktop necessities don't have to look like they came from an office supply store. Here, cans wrapped with scrapbook papers become inexpensive storage containers that complement the decor. Finish them off with a fun scrapbooking embellishment or charm.**

FILED AWAY

above **Plentiful storage is key to keeping a home office looking good, but that doesn't mean settling for boring bins and binders. Boost style and color by decoupaging the fronts of plain bins and magazine holders using scrapbook papers. With a pack of coordinating papers, you can create a mixed yet matched look for less than $10.**

laundry rooms | looks we love

The latest spin on the laundry room has it tidied up and full of style. These freshened-up taskmasters inspire ideas, whether your laundry is a full-fledged room or a sliver of space.

EASY ACCESS

above left **Tucked into cabinetry, a washer and dryer can be out of sight but still close at hand—perfect for a busy kitchen or a back entrance. Yellow cabinets keep this space on the cheerful side. Just close the doors and your laundry area disappears.**

CURTAIN CALL

above right **It's "now you see it, now you don't" for this curtained laundry area carved from space off an upstairs hallway. Gingham curtains hide the utility without the hard look of doors. Stacked machines free room for a sink and drying rack—and are a great way to get more out of a snug space such as a closet or alcove.**

STEPPING BACK

opposite left **Vintage style with modern function is the winning formula in this laundry room. The sink calls to mind an old washtub, and a vintage wire basket makes it easy to tote supplies. The wheeled hamper that plays off the red-and-white-checked floor adds to the old-style look.**

CALL TO ORDER

opposite right **Organization rules in this simply decorated laundry room. Wicker baskets tidy up shelves and hold items such as laundry supplies and just-folded towels. Stenciled numbers on the fronts add a fun touch, along with a reminder of what's stored where. A fabric-covered bulletin board offers a handy place to hang the dog leash and other items that tend to creep into utility rooms.**

laundry room style boosts

Even for workday chores such as laundry, create a space where you want to be. Chores will seem less a drudge, and a tidy space also saves time. Store with style. Items from compotes to serving trays and plastic ice tubs for summer picnics can pull duty as storage. Keep in mind that easy-to-wash containers and bins, rather than fabric ones, work best in a laundry area. Dress up the floor. An indoor-outdoor rug that resists moisture and stains is a simple way to dress up—or even define—a laundry space. In a basement, painting cement floors (or brick walls) beige or white instead of the standard gray instantly brightens. Simplify sorting. Use color-coded hampers or baskets for lights and darks. Having one white and one black laundry basket makes it crystal-clear to everyone where to toss dirty clothes.

laundry rooms | style lessons

Sure, a laundry has to function well, but it can still look good. This vintage-inspired space is loaded with simple ideas for meshing looks and practicality.

WORKING IT
A beaded-board cabinet camouflaging the machines offers a surface for folding clothes. The countertop is inexpensive vinyl flooring. A kitchen island provides more work space.

CLEAN SWEEP

above left **Clear jars store detergents so busy-looking packaging doesn't visually clutter the room. Elsewhere, stain removers go for a spin on a kitchen turntable, and the iron cools off on an enamel tray (a half-sheet cookie tray works, too).**

WASHDAY DECOR

above right **Decorative touches make a laundry room welcoming. Here, framed photos of laundry-related items are inexpensive art; on another wall, photos clamp into pants hangers.**

BRANCHING OUT

right **A vintage drying rack with arms that fold in when it's not being used ups the room's old-school appeal.**

laundry rooms | before & after

Shift a laundry room from boring to fun—and boost its function too. Moving a few things around and adding happy color work wonders.

BEFORE

3 common flaws

1 Inefficient storage creates a messy look.

2 The dryer is isolated from folding space.

3 Personality? It's sorely (and sadly) missing.

AFTER

3 fabulous fixes

1 Shelves solve storage woes; pretty containers get a grip on clutter.

2 Removing the wall-spanning counter improves function and frees up floor space for the ironing board.

3 Color, color, color!

FACE OFF

Moving the washer and dryer so they face one another establishes a mini work core between them. Fabric shirred onto self-adhesive towel bars pretties up the sides of the machines, and a small piece of laminated countertop installed over the dryer creates a folding surface. Use brackets to attach the countertop to the wall, then add a small wooden leg to support the corner. Peel-and-stick carpet squares update the floor and can be individually popped up and replaced if needed.

Try this!
Hang a pretty light fixture to give a work space unexpected sparkle.

WALLS THAT WOW
A graphic accent wall brings fun style to the room, the silhouetted shapes visually balancing with the ironing board on the opposite wall. This design was created by painting over (and then removing) repositionable adhesive-backed paper cut in clothespin shapes and used as stencils. Wall decals are an even easier way to add flair.

SORTED OUT

above left **With labeled baskets, a linen closet shifts into a sorting station that speeds up laundry chores. For drop-and-go ease, the closet door was removed (and hinge holes filled with wood putty before the trim was painted).**

SHOW SOME ID

above right **Painted clothespins become fun label holders, propped in compotes and pretty dishes that serve as storage containers. Use scrapbooking supplies for labels, covering the fronts with clear adhesive-backed paper to waterproof them.**

PRESSING MATTERS

right **Take the guesswork out of what goes where with match-and-stash wall silhouettes. Before painting the wall, trace the ironing board, iron, and supplies onto the back of repositionable adhesive-backed paper to create a stencil. Adhere the cut shapes to the wall. Paint the wall. Remove the paper before the paint dries to reveal the silhouettes. (If your existing wall isn't white or a color you want to be visible, paint the silhouette area before adhering the cut shapes.) To make your ironing board fit the new scheme, spray-paint the legs and use iron-on adhesive web to attach complementary fabric to the cover.**

For projects from kids' art to your own scrapbooking, hobby spaces are in demand these days. Here's how to get crafty and turn a space into your in-home creative getaway.

TWO SIDES

above left **Furniture placement makes all the difference in function. Placing this table perpendicular to the wall creates an easy-access two-sided work space. A settee upholstered in a cheery purple check gives the area banquette-inspired coziness. A cabinet with chalkboard-painted doors and a shelf fitted with cups for markers and scissors keep supplies in reach.**

INDOOR OUTDOOR

above right **This multipurpose crafts room has the easy-care functionality of a mudroom. Quartz-surfacing countertops and walls covered with subway tiles easily wipe clean. An extra-deep double farmhouse sink stylishly handles messes—from arranging flowers to making modeling clay. Shelves keep supplies handy.**

SEWING STATION

opposite left **A desk takes the place of a utilitarian sewing table in this compact hobby corner. A slim hutch on top provides space to keep threads, cut fabrics, and scissors orderly. On the wall, trims stay organized in jars suspended from ribbons wrapped around decorative curtain rods. (The ribbon loops through holes poked in the metal lids.)**

TIDY HIDEAWAY

opposite right **A mini getaway for stamping, scrapbooking, and card-making hides behind closet doors. A hollow-core door that serves as the desktop attaches to a wall-mount rail system, which also supports the shelves. An up-high purple skirt adds cottage prettiness; it hides the original pole bracket and shelf left in place so the space can easily convert back to a conventional closet if needed.**

hobby areas on a budget

Gaining room for hobbies doesn't require building a backyard getaway. Here are three ways to find space without spending a fortune. Work with what you have. An armoire that doesn't fit the new flat-panel TV can be turned into a hobby zone. Outfit the insides with stackable cubbies with drawers. Adhere corkboard to the insides of cabinet doors to use as an inspiration board. If a dark finish seems too serious, paint the armoire a fun color. Rearrange furniture. Sometimes you simply have to move things around to make room for what you really want. In a guest bedroom, scoot a twin bed up to the wall and add pillows so it looks like a daybed, then claim the opened-up space as your hobby zone. Use wall space. Rolls of wrapping paper slipped onto decorative curtain rods or dowels hung above a cart or small table in a mudroom or basement can launch a colorful gift-wrapping station.

This multitasking room handles it all—crafting, wrapping, homework, laundry—and still looks good doing it.

PRACTICAL MATTERS

The built-in counter-height desktop—used primarily as a kids' art spot—makes it easy to check messages pinned to the corkboard. Slate countertops look similar to soapstone common to old cottages but require less maintenance. Barn-style doors are a fun way to hide the contents of the storage closets.

Barn-style doors, a painted floor, and yellow cabinets add character.

WRAP AND GO
top left **The key to staying organized is to give everything its own home. In the island, drawers are sized for specific items, such as a long shallow drawer for rolls of wrapping paper.**

ON THE SURFACE
top right **The painted floor adds fun pattern—and practicality. With its distressed finish, dirt is less noticeable.**

CRAFTING CARRYALL
middle left **Handled containers make it easy to tote art supplies wherever they're needed. This basket earns organizational bonus points for its dividers.**

OLD-TIME STORAGE
bottom left **A vintage wine-bottle dryer organizes spools of ribbons. Chalkboard tags on the woven baskets make labeling a breeze.**

KID-FRIENDLY BINS
far right **Colorful translucent bins make it easy to see what's stored in them—perfect for kids to grab what they need. Adjustable shelves keep the storage space flexible.**

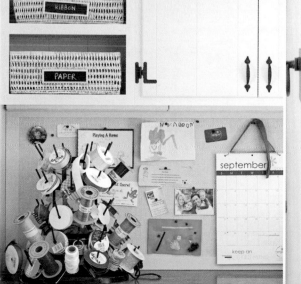

Creative storage and work-space-stretching ideas ensure that this L-shape hobby zone is pretty enough to slip into any corner.

CRAFTY CORNER

An abundance of creamy white furniture and shelves keeps this corner hobby area light, bright, and cottage cute. Two bookshelves hold a piece of painted wood to create a work space long enough to accommodate crafting and wrapping. Shelves and a cabinet make use of vertical space and allow easy access to supplies. With curved brackets and thick molding detailing the shelves, along with glass doors and beaded-board on the cabinet, the pieces display plenty of style.

WELL COMPOSED

below A hobby room needs places to tack up inspirational ideas and notes without looking messy. This wall collage beautifully mixes functional and pretty items. A magnetic board and clipboard used to hold photos or notes address the room's practical requirements, while a mirror and framed photos pretty up the composition.

CLEVERLY RETASKED

right Look for storage pieces that do more than, well, just store. A tiered kitchen stand used as a catchall for bows adds vintage charm. A lunch box—old or new—is a fun way to gain closed storage. With cubbies and pegs for hanging things, the beaded-board cabinet is ideal for keeping supplies sorted. (Surprise! It's intended for a bathroom.)

notebook

Looking for ways to bring a little (or a lot) of cottage flair to your home? Our hands-on projects and inspiring ideas do the trick—simply and affordably.

Cottage style welcomes creativity—with vintage items or new ones. These simple ideas bring conversation-starting character to every room of the house.

1 ON A ROLL Repurpose a vintage suitcase into a charming underbed catchall that's perfect for storing notepads, letters, and magazines. Attach casters to holes drilled in the bottom. Remove the top, and add a fabric cover for easy access.

2 PHOTO GALLERY Old oars or paddles make a perfect photo perch in a beach cottage. Screw metal hooks into each oar to create mini ledges for frames to rest on. Roughed-up frames complement the weathered display.

3 MAIL STOP Shift a discarded birdcage into a sorting center for mail and stationery. Scrub the cage with a bleach solution. Clip off wires from the front and back, leaving a few to create mail slots. For shelves, cut dowel rods slightly longer than the cage width and notch the wood to help it grab the wires. Cut glass or Plexiglas shelves to fit, and place them on the dowel rods.

4 CURTAIN CALL Let tea towels step out as sweet and simple café curtains. Install a curtain rod at the center of the window, then attach curtain clips to the towels and hang them from the rod. If your tea towels are too long, add a no-sew hem using fusible webbing and an iron.

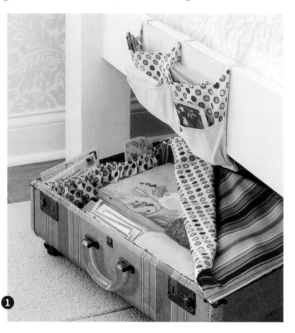

MESSAGE BOARD

Cleaned, sanded, and painted, a rustic garage door panel becomes a clever and versatile art piece. Bulldog clips from an office supply store hang from screws to suspend decorations, photos, kids' artworks—or you name it—that drop down into the windowed panes. For special occasions such as holidays or birthdays, print letters in a decorative font or enlarge them from a clip art book and spell out a message.

furniture facelifts

Tired of run-of-the-mill furniture? These quick pick-me-ups add big personality and a custom look without much effort or expense.

TRIMMED OUT

An old table looks fresh and flirty when trimmed with old-style wooden clothespins and painted sunny yellow. Dab wood glue onto the back of a clothespin. Press the clothespin against the table edge, with its top about ½ inch above the tabletop, then nail it into place at its chubbiest part using a pneumatic pin nailer. Repeat around the tabletop edge. To keep the clothespins level as you work, place a ½-inch-thick board on the tabletop to use as an alignment guide.

1 BACK STORY

Wallpaper the back of a cabinet for a custom look that ties into the room's color scheme and to give displayed items more prominence. For an easy-to-remove treatment or for cabinets that don't have removable shelves, wallpaper pieces of foam-core board cut to fit the spaces, and place those between shelves.

2 WELL DRESSED

For a soft flourish and hidden storage, skirt a console table with store-bought café curtains. Embellish the curtains with ribbon or a strip of scrap fabric. Use tension rods to hang the curtains between the table legs.

3 WAKE-UP CALL

Furniture makeovers don't get much easier than this: Simply drape a rug over a tired old headboard for a soft and pretty new look. Choose a lightweight woven rug that's slightly narrower than the headboard. To keep the rug in place, use pairs of clip-on curtain rings (four rings for each side) tied together with ribbon.

4 TAKE A NUMBER

Add a little flair to dining chairs with house numbers. Paint mismatched chairs to unify them, then nail house numbers to the chair backs with wide slats for a just-for-fun touch.

painted-on character

Work wonders on just about anything with a little paint (and a stencil here and there). Surfaces that once looked flat will be full of life.

1 COLOR BLOCKED

Give sisal—a cottage favorite—new attitude with paint. Use painter's tape and a straightedge to mask off squares and rectangles on a sisal rug. Dip a flat trimming brush into interior semigloss paint; pounce the brush vertically to cover each section. Work paint into the fibers and along the painter's tape edges.

2 DRESSY DRESSER

Sassy color and easy-to-add pattern perk up any hand-me-down. This bedside dresser limits a chicken-wire-inspired stencil design to the top drawer for impact. Use a stencil brush to dab a small amount of paint over the stencil. For a subtle design, use paint that's one shade darker than the base color.

3 A STEP ABOVE

Stenciled stairs deliver a look that's classic yet fresh. For ease, use an oversize stencil; this one was about 3 feet wide, but the edges were taped off to reduce the width.

4 SKETCH A LOOK

Paint is the easiest way to update kitchen cabinets. For depth, paint the recessed panels of upper cabinets a darker shade than the rest of the cabinetry. Hand-paint simple kitchen motifs in the centers of panels—the imperfections of the lines add to the charm.

paint a plaid floor

Make the floor the star of your porch with a classic design.

Do the prep work. Prime the clean floor; let dry. Purchase floor paint in white and two shades of blue. (For this porch, an exterior floor-and-deck paint was used.) With a roller, paint the floor white; let dry.

Mark it off. Use a pencil, a long board, and a tape measure to mark 14-inch squares on the entire floor. Map out the color sequence on paper, referring to the photo. Using painter's tape, mask off squares that will get the first blue color. Align the tape along the *outside* of each square, so the interior squares remain a full 14 inches. Press the tape to the floor.

Begin painting. Use a roller to paint the taped-off squares. Immediately remove the tape and wipe up any bleeding paint with a rag; let dry. Repeat for the second blue color. The white base will create the remaining squares. This project will take up to four days for proper drying.

CHECKED OUT

An oversize blue-and-white plaid painted onto the floor gives this porch a big dose of cottage style. Two shades of blue alternate atop a white base to create the timeless pattern.

outdoor decor

Do your outdoor spaces seem to lack a little something? These quick spruce-ups will splash them with color, character, and interest.

1 SWEET POSY An outdoor bouquet offers a sweet little surprise for anyone who walks your way. Contain flowers and foliage—hosta leaves add great color and texture— in a vintage watering can. Hang on a picket fence, door, or hook.

2 SLEEK WORK SPACE A stainless-steel kitchen cart makes a sleek-looking potting bench (or a nifty buffet) on a porch or patio. Hang shelves above, displaying items you need to have handy along with a few decorative pieces that add interest.

3 PRETTIED UP Bring an indoor accent table onto the porch for a touch of class. Use canning jars as casual vases for carefree bouquets. Other ways to add comfort: a mirror (add a chain or ribbon to the back, and hang from a hook) and pillows—use ones made from outdoor fabric for the most longevity.

4 LEMON ZEST Rethink a galvanized lantern as a quick and easy tabletop decoration. Simply place a lemon or other citrus fruit inside the center for a pop of summer color and a no-watering-needed centerpiece. Group several lanterns on a dining table, or spread them around a porch.

PERFECT SETTING

Set the scene for a backyard picnic under a big old tree. Define the dining area with an outdoor rug or a picnic blanket. A weathered table and mismatched chairs pulled from around the house and porch add character. Twine-suspended bottles, each filled with a geranium cutting, dress the chair backs. For the hanging luminarias, use a crafts knife (and a stencil if you want) to cut designs in a paper grocery bag. Wrap around small lanterns outfitted with handles and votive candles, and hang with twine from tree branches, away from foliage.

wicker makeovers

Wicker is quintessential cottage, beloved indoors and out. For a change of pace from classic white, update your pieces with fun color or fabrics.

1 TRIMMED OUT

A bright border applied with an artist's brush and crafts paint gives any piece of wicker a new look. Gingham dish towels wrapped around cushions add charm. Thread ribbon through holes made in the towels with a grommet punch, and tie around a cushion or to the chair to hold in place. Embellish towels with rickrack and trims.

2 GOING IN CIRCLES

Mirror a chair's rounded form with perky polka dots. For the base coat, spray the chair medium green. When dry, brush with lighter green crafts paint for a shadowy effect. Stencil circles randomly onto the chair.

3 SPRING FLING

Swap background and stencil colors to craft a cheerful coordinated set. Spray-paint a primed wicker table white and a primed chair yellow. When dry, spray-paint the table rim yellow. Stencil daisies and dots on the top, using spray paints; switch the colors for the chair. Add details with an artist's brush and crafts paints.

4 BRIGHT SPOT

Refresh a room by bringing an outdoor piece indoors. Painted kiwi and plumped with a cushion, pillow, and throw, this wicker chair fits right in with a modern scheme.

refresh wicker

A fresh coat of paint can juice up any piece of wicker—a chair, a table, or a basket.

Prep it. Clean wicker that's been outdoors by spraying it with a garden hose. Lightly sand, and rub the piece with a tack cloth. Use a wire brush to remove loose paint.

Assess your pieces. Newer wicker-look pieces tend to be made of resin; use a primer designed for plastic and acrylic paint. For a natural wicker piece, use oil-base paint.

Spray on color. Spray paint penetrates wicker's crevices, unlike brushed-on paint, which tends to glob. Spray several thin coats, rather than one heavy one. Instead of white, choose a fun color such as yellow or lime. Or use a metallic silver spray paint for a sleek look.

SWEETLY TAILORED

Soft embellishments turn a wicker chair into a dreamy dressing table companion. For the skirt, sew a basting stitch along the tops of store-bought valances, gather the valances, and hot-glue them around the bottom of the seat frame. Use an old chenille bedspread or robe as a cushion cover, and a bed pillow for a backrest. Finish with a bolster wrapped with a shawl and a handkerchief tied with ribbon.

There's no reason to let walls go bare. Whether you use maps picked up on a vacation or rolls of wallpaper, art is easier to come by than you might think.

1 MAP IT OUT

Framing a map—new or vintage—is an easy way to personalize a room and highlight your journeys. Here, a vintage Cape Cod map adds beachy style that links to an aqua pottery collection.

2 SERVE UP STYLE

Take the timeless idea of hanging plates on a wall a step further by letting a tray go solo as an art piece. This round tray adds fun pattern, and its shape plays off the table. For texture, hang a single woven tray or group several.

3 COLLECTIVE DISPLAY

Get the look of big art with a collage of small items—perfect for that tough-to-fill wall space above a sofa. For variety, hang round or oval objects, such as plates and a small mirror, with rectangular pieces. If you want dimension, add a wall bracket to the grouping, and top it with a small vase. Test your arrangement on the floor before hanging it.

4 SCRAP ART

Wondering what to do with a piece of leftover fabric that's too pretty to toss? Frame it! Paint an old wooden picture frame, cut foam-core board to fit the opening, and cover the board with the fabric.

PAPERED BACKDROP

Turn wallpaper into an easy-to-hang, easy-to-change accent behind a bed. Simply cut three equal-size lengths of wallpaper, then hang them from bulldog clips, slipping the clips over small nails in the wall. Change the look seasonally—or whenever you want—using remnants from a store or leftovers from one of your projects.

finishing touches

The little things make a big difference in any room. Personalize your spaces with displays that show your personality and interests.

BOOK IT Looking for a simple way to add style to a side table? Simply grab a few of your favorite books. Stack them on the table, and top with a small bouquet of fresh flowers. (For the most impact, use same-color flowers.) Books add personality to any space, and stacking them gives small items—flowers, a seashell, an alarm clock—a boost.

1 CUTE CLUSTER
Old bottles create an everyday centerpiece that's great for showing off garden clippings—and that's more interesting than a standard vase. Contain small bottles in a vintage milk or soda carrier.

2 COLLECTIVE DISPLAY
Show off a collection of hats by hanging them on a wall. These straw hats add texture and complement the brownish hues of the dresser and mirror.

3 SERVING A PURPOSE
Consider a serving tray one of your most-valued accessories; anything displayed on it will look more pulled together. Here, a weathered wooden tray holds a bowl of seashells and rocks on a coffee table. Trays are also versatile—use them in a bedroom for jewelry and accessories or in a kitchen as a mail stop. For a small surface, use a bathroom tray; it's a handy organizer for TV remotes and small items such as reading glasses.

4 MEMORIES IN A BOTTLE
Bag some sand from trips to the beach, and use it to fill old apothecary bottles. Grouped on a mantel or shelf, the bottles create a 3-D scrapbook. Add labels to ensure you'll recall the when and where.

PHOTO CREDITS

page 14
Stylist, Stacy Kunstel
Photographer, Michael Partinio

page 30
Field editor, Andrea Caughey
Stylist, Char Hatch Langos
Photographer, Edmund Barr

page 78
Field editor and Stylist: Sarah Alba
Photographer: Paul Dyer

Page 88
Field editor and stylist, Sandi Mohlmann
Photographer: Andreas Trauttmansdorff

page 122
Field editor and stylist, Sandi Mohlmann
Photographer, Richard Leo Johnson

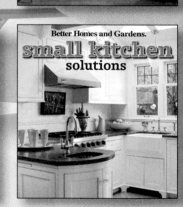

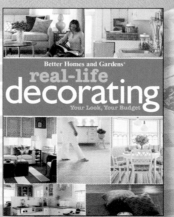
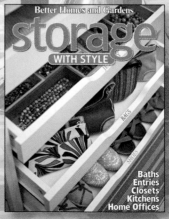
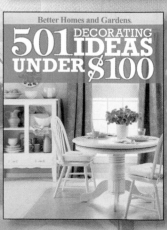